Gavin Turner

A Century at Bath

OVER ONE HUNDRED YEARS OF
SOMERSET COUNTY CRICKET AT THE REC

BROADCAST BOOKS

ACKNOWLEDGEMENTS

For allowing me to use numerous extracts and photographs from
their newspapers, I wish to extend my thanks to
Bath Newspapers and their Editor.
Quotations from Wisden's Cricketers' Almanack are reproduced by
kind permission of John Wisden & Co. Ltd.
Quotations from The Times Newspaper are © Times Newspapers
Limited, 8 May 1923 and 16 June 1987.
The Article by Neville Cardus in Chapter 17 is reproduced by
kind permission of Margaret Hughes.

For their help in connection with this book, I wish particularly to thank
Stephen Green, Glenys Williams and Michael Wolton of the Marylebone
Cricket Club, Tony Stedall of the Somerset Cricket Museum,
Michael Hill, President of Somerset CCC, and Robert Appleyard,
Adrian Burton, Michael Davis, Max Jeffrey and Colonel Ted Lewis,
all of Somerset CCC and the Friends of Bath County Cricket Festival,
and all those, many of whom are named herein, who have courteously
granted me interviews for this book.

In addition to the Bath Chronicle and other newspapers, the following
have been invaluable in connection with the research for this book:
(a) The Annual Wisden Cricketers' Almanacks;
(b) Who's Who of Cricketers: Philip Bailey, Philip Thorn and Peter
Wynne-Thomas; Hamlyn: London, 1984, Rev 1993, in association with
The Association of Cricket Statisticians and Historians.
(c) Somerset CCC First Class Records 1882-1995: Ed Nigel Johns.

I would also like to acknowledge the help which I have received from
two histories, Donald Bradfield's 'The Lansdown Story' and
Peter Roebuck's 'From Sammy to Jimmy – The Official History of
Somerset County Cricket Club'.

This book has been produced with the approval and encouragement of
the Bath and Wiltshire Area Committee of
Somerset County Cricket Club
to celebrate over one hundred years of county cricket at the Rec.

TABLE OF CONTENTS

Chapter 1   INTRODUCTION   5

Chapter 2   CRICKET IN BATH BEFORE THE REC.   9

Chapter 3   FESTIVAL CRICKET AND SOCIETY   14

Chapter 4   FOUR MEMORABLE SOMERSET VICTORIES   21

Chapter 5   THE GOLDEN AGE   28

Chapter 6   FOUR IMPRESSIVE PERSONAL ACHIEVEMENTS   33

Chapter 7   AMATEURS, PROFESSIONALS AND BENEFITS   38

Chapter 8   THE GREAT AUSTRALIAN CRICKET TRADITION   45

Chapter 9   MORE OVERSEAS CRICKETERS   50

Chapter 10   BETWEEN THE WARS   57

Chapter 11   SOMERSET PERSONALITIES FROM BATH   65

Chapter 12   CATCHES WIN MATCHES   70

Chapter 13   THE RECREATION GROUND   75

Chapter 14   SETTING UP THE FESTIVAL   80

Chapter 15   THE LAST HALF-CENTURY   86

Chapter 16   LIMITED OVERS CRICKET   94

Chapter 17   'FOUR MORE GERANIA, CRUSOE'   99

Chapter 18   'CURIOUSER AND CURIOUSER'   102

Appendix 1   SOMERSET FIRST-CLASS MATCHES AT BATH   109

Appendix 2   SOMERSET LIMITED OVERS MATCHES AT BATH   113

ILLUSTRATION ACKNOWLEDGEMENTS   114

INDEX   115

Somerset v *Australia; Bath, May 1977.*

CHAPTER 1

INTRODUCTION

IN 1894, the Bath and County Recreation Ground Company Limited was formed to supply the city with an adequate athletic ground. The land acquired for this purpose was Pulteney Meadows including that part known as the Spring Gardens, or Vauxhall Gardens, a site which had been used, since the middle of the eighteenth century, for many a public breakfast and pleasure party. The grounds were accordingly laid out and by the turn of the century, the Recreation Ground, or the 'Rec', as it is always known, became the home of Bath Football Club, the original name of the city's famous rugby club, and for one or two weeks of the summer, of Somerset County Cricket Club.

Somerset's first match on the Rec started on Monday 19 July 1897 and was played against the Philadelphians, a touring team of amateurs from the United States of America, whose matches that season in England were accorded first-class status.

The first county cricket match played on the Rec was on 16-18 May 1898, when Somerset met Yorkshire. Every year since then, apart from those wartime years when no first-class cricket was played, there has been a Somerset County Cricket Festival at the Rec. During that time, some 250 first-class matches have been scheduled for Bath; every first-class county playing cricket in England (except Durham, who joined the championship only in 1992) has visited Bath, as have also sides from both Oxford and Cambridge Universities, and International Touring Teams from Australia, New Zealand, Pakistan, South Africa, and West Indies (all over here to play Test Matches against England). From 1969, limited overs games played by Somerset against other first-class counties have also been included in the Festival (47 so far, plus one against Buckinghamshire). Appendices at the end of the book contain brief details of all matches played at the Rec.

Over the years, what started in 1898 as a Cricket Week (Monday to Saturday) in May has changed its format many times. Although the Festival has been held mainly in June, Somerset matches have also been played in Bath in May, July and August, on one occasion (1961) ending in September. Four matches a season were frequently played at the Rec, usually split between two weeks at different times of the summer. With the arrival of the limited overs game into English professional cricket, at least one such match has since 1969 featured as part of the Bath Cricket Festival. Now that the three day match has been replaced by one of four days' duration, the Festival has since 1993 comprised one county championship match and one limited overs game.

There are older county cricket festivals than that at Bath; those at Canterbury and Cheltenham to name just two. All festivals, with their unique atmosphere, have added to the pleasure of the game, and importantly have spread its appeal more widely around the country. It is at festivals that cricket finds its roots and where the true soul of the game resides. Over the years, spectators at Bath have been privileged to see, representing Somerset or their visitors, some of the finest cricketers ever to play the game.

This book makes no claim to be a comprehensive history; it is a miscellany, written to celebrate the varied aspects and achievements of the Bath Cricket Festival and to recognise the contribution of those people, mostly volunteers, whose love of the game has ensured that county cricket has been played in Bath now for over 100 years, thus providing the city of Bath with one more festival to

One of the two elegant turnstiles at the Great Pulteney Street end.

6

While preparing the publicity for the 2001 Festival, Marcus Trescothick takes time off to give some
slip-catching practice to Earl Moorhouse, Michael Davis, Amanda Gilmer and Bob Holder.

celebrate, and its visitors with one more attraction to enjoy.

That the Festival has continued as long as it has might be regarded as (to borrow from Dr Johnson) 'a triumph of hope over experience', but will the Bath Cricket Festival survive in the future? The Recreation Ground is not a purpose-built cricket ground, and the costs of setting it up for cricket each year mount. There is no doubt that the changes to the format of the County Championship in the 1990s and the consequent reduced allocation of matches to Bath has greatly diminished the potential of the Festival to make a profit. The proportion of Somerset members in and around Bath has correspondingly declined. In the 1960s, the Bath Area membership regularly amounted to 20 per cent of the total Somerset membership. In the year 2000, with nearly 500 out of 7,000 members, the figure is nearer to 7 per cent. As the organisation and structure of cricket in Britain becomes more commercial, finance and moves towards increasing centralisation tend to dominate all thoughts.

The historian must, however, note that the Festival has been threatened in the past and has always survived. The Somerset County Cricket Club Chairman, Richard Parsons and the Vice-Chairman, Robert Appleyard are both enthusiastic supporters of the Festival. There is also a strong argument that some small part of the large

7

annual distribution which Somerset receives (as do all other first-class counties) from the England and Wales Cricket Board central finance pool, derived mainly from Test Match receipts, the sale of TV and broadcasting rights, marketing and sponsorships, should be applied towards maintaining festival cricket.

Bath has been allocated a Festival for June 2001, when Yorkshire will be the visitors, one of the most popular fixtures in the cricket calendar. The Bath and North East Somerset Council has agreed in principle to continue its support of the Festival for a further three year period; and in March 2001 a very generous sponsorship of the Festival by Bath solicitors Withy King was announced. The outlook for the continuation of the Festival is thus brighter than it has been for many years. Cricket lovers in Bath are nevertheless encouraged to follow the advice of the Latin poet Horace: '*Carpe diem*' (enjoy the present). Let us enjoy the Festival while we may.

CHAPTER 2

Cricket in Bath Before the Rec

'Here lies Fred
Who was alive and is dead;
If it had been his father
I would much rather;
If it had been his brother,
Still better than another;
If it had been his sister
No one would have missed her
If it had been the whole generation,
So much better for the nation;
But as it's only Fred,
Who was alive and is dead,
Why, there's nothing more to be said'.

In Bath, Frederick Prince of Wales, eldest son and heir of King George II and father of King George III, was welcomed and admired much more than the Anti-Hanoverian sentiments, expressed in the doggerel verse above, would suggest. In 1738, an obelisk was erected in his honour in the centre of Queen Square and Alexander Pope was prevailed upon to write the inscription. It reads: 'In Memory of honours conferred and in gratitude for benefits bestowed in this city by His Royal Highness Frederick, Prince of Wales and his Royal Consort in the Year 1738, this Obelisk is erected by Richard Nash Esq'.

Frederick was an admirer of cricket and a player, albeit of modest talent, and his untimely death in 1751 may have been caused indirectly by a blow to the

9

Bath: a cricket ground in the mid-nineteenth century; watercolour by Felix (Nicholas Wanostrocht).

head from a cricket ball – although Horace Walpole asserted that a tennis ball was the culprit. The importance of Frederick to cricket in Bath lies in the fact that it was in his honour that the first recorded game of cricket there was played. The Bath Journal reports that on Saturday 13 July 1751 'there was a great Cricket Match in Sal[t]ford-Meadow, about four miles below this City, in Memory of his late Royal Highness the Prince of Wales'. On a visit to Bath in the previous year Frederick, accompanied by his wife and attended by several noblemen and ladies, had dined in public in a meadow at Saltford. Following his death the cricket match was played in the same place on the anniversary of his visit.

Cricket matches were also reported played in the eighteenth century on Claverton Down and many will doubtless have participated in informal games, such as those liked by Jane Austen's youthful heroine, Catherine Morland, before she came to Bath.

It is however in the nineteenth century that the game became more structured and more firmly entrenched in the city with the formation of both the Bath and the Lansdown Clubs, the latter starting in 1825. E.M.Grace captained the club, G.F.Grace also played for them, and their more famous brother, Dr. W.G.Grace made numerous appearances for Lansdown between 1861 and 1882. During the same period W.G., playing for West Gloucestershire, Clifton, Bedminster and others, appeared equally frequently against the Lansdown club. Even before the Grace brothers were playing regularly, Lansdown had hosted matches involving some of the most talented cricketers in the country. Among the teams playing were the celebrated All England XI, including William Clarke, George Parr, Felix (a talented water-colourist as well as a fine cricketer) and others who took on XXII of Lansdown in 1852. This was the first of eight fixtures between these two teams played over a thirteen year period at Lansdown's old Sydenham Field (Lower Bristol Road) ground.

The most remarkable match to be played in Bath in the mid-nineteenth century took place in August 1845 when the Western Counties, including Fuller Pilch, Thomas Box (the wicketkeeper) and Alfred Mynn played the Marylebone Cricket Club at Lansdown's old Racecourse ground. Pilch, the greatest batsman of his day, scored 117 (out of 248) and Alfred Mynn's bowling was largely responsible for the dismissal of MCC for 56 and 97. The performances on the cricket ground, outstanding though some of them were, have been largely overshadowed by events immediately after the match. The Bath Chronicle of 21 August 1845 reported as follows:

All England XI v XXII of Lansdown, 1863. Number 12 is a youthful Dr. W.G. Grace.

11

'At the conclusion of the game, a somewhat strange circumstance created a considerable degree of excitement. A Sheriff's Officer, accompanied by Mr. W.P.Hall, Mayor's Officer, appeared on the Down with a very ominous piece of paper, in the shape of a warrant for taking the person of Mr. Mynn, or obtaining from him about £130, owing by him to some creditor in London. The parties arrived on the ground at about one o'clock, but it was arranged that Mr. Mynn should not be disturbed till the conclusion of the game, but that then he should surrender himself. When the last wicket was drawn, the players retreated to their cottage, Mr. Mynn being followed closely by the Officers, who kept their man in view. However, Mr Mynn got into the cottage and a number of his friends placed themselves in the doorway, and effectually prevented the officers from entering. The upshot of the matter was that one of Mr. Mynn's friends undertook to pay the money or to deliver Mr. Mynn to the Sheriff's officer last night'.

Although the Bath Chronicle concluded that it had 'not heard which course was taken', it is assumed that his friends were unable to find the required amount of money for Alfred Mynn was reported shortly afterwards to be in jail.

A team representing Somerset encountered both Dorset and Devonshire at Lansdown in 1871 but it was in the 1880s that Somerset, which had been formed as a county cricket club in 1875, began to play some county matches in Bath at the ground of the Lansdown club. Somerset's continuous status as a first-class cricket county started in 1891 but it had been recognised as a first-class county during an earlier period (1882- 85) and in August 1884, Somerset achieved a memorable victory against Hampshire at Bath, Somerset's sole win in that season of six matches played on a home and away basis against Hampshire, Kent and Lancashire.

In his history of the Lansdown Club 'The Lansdown Story', Donald Bradfield claims that Bath's first county cricket week occurred at Lansdown in the week of 14 to 20 July 1881, when Somerset had matches against Gloucestershire (including W.G. Grace and E.M. Grace, who scored 80 and 52 respectively) and Hampshire. This was, however, not only just one isolated week in the decade, but also before Somerset achieved first-class status. Thus the annual Somerset County Cricket Festival at Bath, which has been continuous since 1897, apart from wartime, really began with the laying down of the ground at the Rec.

The directors of the Recreation Ground Company always wanted county cricket to be played on their ground. In the winter of 1894-5, a cricket pitch was laid down there under the supervision of George Hearne, a member of a well-known

Alfred Mynn, oil painting by William Bromley, c.1850.

family of cricket professionals from South East England. After a two year period of preparation, the Somerset County Committee, in order to test out the ground and pitch, awarded to the Rec the match to be played against a visiting team from the United States, the Philadelphians. Thus it was that on Monday 19 July 1897, the Somerset County Cricket team, captained by Sammy Woods and including the Palairet brothers, and the professionals Nicholls, Tyler and Robson, entertained the Philadelphian team. The visitors, who were all amateurs, were not the most talented of cricketers in England that summer, and the match was affected by rain and ended in a draw. The ground receipts for the whole match totalled £72 and it was estimated that on the Tuesday some 1500 spectators were in the Rec. This was sufficient encouragement to the Somerset Committee to arrange some county matches at the Rec for 1898.

There were probably other reasons. Even though most of the Somerset cricketers were amateurs, expenses were still incurred, and attendances at matches at Taunton, where the County Ground was situated, were poor. A move of some matches away from Taunton would also allow cricket lovers from other parts of the County to see the first-class game.

CHAPTER 3

FESTIVAL CRICKET AND SOCIETY

A FESTIVAL IS SUPPOSED TO BE A JOYFUL OCCASION. A cricket festival should be a celebration of the pleasures of the game and of the opportunity given to spectators from a particular town or region, for one or two weeks of the year, to enjoy the experience of watching first-class cricket. As long ago as 1908, references can be found to 'excursionists' coming to Bath for the cricket Festival. But it is not simply the opportunity to watch the cricket against the backdrop of the famous Abbey and the honey-coloured stone buildings of the Georgian city, or to see the elegant Palladian façade of Prior Park on the hillside above, which brings spectators to Bath. There is also the very special atmosphere of the Festival and the opportunity which it gives to indulge those two lasting characteristics of a visit to Bath, meeting people and socialising. This was what Richard 'Beau' Nash, the Master of Ceremonies here in the first half of the eighteenth century had worked hard to promote, and his legacy endures.

The Bath Cricket Festival, like the international music festival which usually precedes it, is an eagerly awaited event, an annual celebration, around the dates of which holidays are planned. Edward Francis is one who has been regularly visiting Bath for the cricket Festival for over 40 years, Jack Blanchard is another, having been taken by his father to his first Festival in 1950; and David and Janet Ball of Bathford have been taking a week's holiday for the Bath Cricket Festival for over 40 years, their second week being reserved for the annual Somerset cricket festival at Weston-Super-Mare until its recent demise; these are just a few of those who regularly come to the Rec.

Right from the beginning, the social aspect of the Bath Cricket Festival has been important. Marquee tents have featured on the Rec from the earliest days.

A marquee and enclosure at the Bath Cricket Festival, 1902.

Another strong supporter of the Festival, Colonel Ted Lewis remembered his mother talking about accompanying her father to the Bath and County Club's marquee in the early 1900s when Len Braund was regarded as the finest Somerset player and Sammy Woods and Lionel Palairet would chat to the guests there between innings. These three legendary figures from Somerset's history all scored centuries for the County at Bath.

The July 1901 edition of the 'Bath and County Graphic' reported that what 'proved an attractive feature in regard to the [Bath Cricket] week were the receptions held by various ladies and gentlemen. This brought together a large number of people who otherwise may not have attended, and the idea can be said to have very materially swelled the attendance. Among the ladies and gentlemen who held receptions were Mrs Fish and Mrs Baxter of Bathhampton; Mrs Morgan of 'Cranhill'; Major Simpson, Captain and Mrs Delaval Astley, and the Bath and County Club. The new arrangement was thoroughly appreciated'. A large gathering also attended Mrs Gwynne James' 'At Home' at the Rec on the first day of the Australia match in 1909.

These private receptions were a regular feature of Bath Cricket Festival Week, although their success, as well as that of the cricket, was dependent upon good weather. A string of cancellations on account of rain caused hostesses to re-think their strategies for entertaining, and these events gradually diminished. However, Mrs Hugh Mostyn was reported as holding a small 'At Home' at the Rec for the first day of the Hampshire match in 1923; and the Marquess of Bath, during his year of office as President of the Club, held a reception for some 500 guests in June 1925, on the first day of Somerset's match against Cambridge University when spectators were treated to an exhibition of brilliant batting by K.S.Duleepsinjhi who scored 130 for the University. The following day, Mrs Richardson and Mrs Sylvester gave an 'At Home' for some 350 guests, the catering for both these functions being in the hands of the well-known Bath caterers, Fortts and Son of Milsom Street.

Following the austerity of wartime and the immediate post-war period, it is pleasing to note that in June 1954 the Mayor of Bath held a reception at the Rec after close of play on the Monday of the Somerset v Middlesex match. Two years earlier, in a match between the same counties, the players had been invited to visit the Mayor's parlour. This time (1954), the players, officials of the county club, members of the local cricket festival committee and several former players were invited to the reception. In his speech of welcome, the Mayor was reported as saying that all in Bath wanted to do everything possible to make the cricket Festival a success. During the match against Australia in 1977, the Mayor of Bath hosted a reception at the Roman Baths for a large gathering including players and officials.

In the last thirty years the marquees have re-appeared at the Festival but the 'At Homes' given by various society ladies in Bath have been replaced by companies offering corporate hospitality to their clients. The support of these firms, many of them local businesses, has been vital to the continuation of the Festival. For many years too, the Somerset Wyverns, a club of enthusiastic Somerset followers based outside the County, and the Lord's Taverners, a body of cricket watchers dedicated to raise funds for various charitable causes, have hired marquees in support of the Festival.

Since 1988, the marquee of the Friends of the Bath County Cricket Festival has been a focal point and haven for those dedicated to maintain the cause of Somerset cricket in Bath. As well as supplying a comfortable view of proceedings on the field of play, the Friends,

Sylvia and Robert Appleyard, Bath Festival 1993.

with over 350 members, provide significant financial support to the Festival. The Friends' objective is to support and encourage the playing of a County Cricket Festival in Bath and the founders of the organisation, Max Jeffrey, Len Creed, and Robert and Sylvia Appleyard have worked tirelessly to this end. With their annual cheese and wine party commencing immediately after close of play on one of the match days, the Friends now under the Chairmanship of Bob Holder, maintain an important social aspect to the Festival.

Throughout their existence, the Friends have received strong support from Alfie Stringer, Ted Lewis, Penny Lewis and Derek and Anne Brown. Another of those stalwarts who has been supporting the Bath Cricket Festival for over 40 years, Derek Brown was a member (Jack Blanchard was another) of an informal group known as the 'friends of Bath Cricket' who regularly met for coffee in the market café and sat together in the members' area during the Festival.

Before the founding of the Friends of Bath, the Somerset County Cricket Club Supporters Club regularly took a marquee at the Bath Festival. This organisation, of which Len Creed was President for many years, provided substantial financial help to Somerset County Cricket Club over a period of more than 40 years until it was wound up in the 1990s. Among its many initiatives was the purchase of a portable stand, for installation at the various grounds around the County where Somerset played cricket. Another, and this was the action of the Bath Branch of the Supporters' Club, was to acquire and instal all the necessary equipment for broadcasting match commentaries from the Rec to the Royal United Hospital in Bath. It was in June 1956, for the match between Somerset and Kent, that the first live broadcast was made, the patients hearing commentaries given by Louis Powell and Bill Andrews.

As well as offering hospitality at the Rec, social events during the Festival have often had the secondary purpose of fund-raising. In 1901, a military tattoo arranged in Royal Victoria Park and attended by about 8,000 persons was accounted a huge success; and as a result, the Bath and County Graphic was happy to report that 'the fund for the ensuring of a cricket week in Bath will greatly benefit'.

The military tattoo was an exceptional event, although there was a similar happening when the band of H.M. Royal Marines Commando Forces arrived to entertain spectators during the lunch and tea intervals on the first two days of the Australian Team's visit in May 1977. Away from the Rec, however, other social occasions during the Festival followed a consistent pattern. Whereas in the rain-affected week of June 1903, the two subscription dances at the Assembly Rooms were poorly attended, the Bath Chronicle of Saturday 22 May 1920 was pleased to record that an 'enjoyable cricket week dance took place at the Bath Spa Hotel on Thursday, dancing commencing at about 8.30 and continuing to 1.30 to the music of the hotel elite orchestra'. After recording the names of those on the committee responsible for the arrangements, the paper reported that among those attending were Mr J.Daniell and Mr A.E.S. Rippon of Somerset CCC, a form of relaxation which undoubtedly will have contributed to Somerset's famous victory over Surrey at the end of that week. The dance too made a profit and the sum of over £5 was donated to the Cricket Week Fund. A Festival Dance continued as one of the regular social occasions of Cricket Week. In the 1950s, nearly 400 people attended the dance, organised by the Bath Branch of the Somerset County Cricket Club Supporters Club. The event, at the Regency Ballroom on 13 June 1956, was for Maurice Tremlett's benefit and was judged by the Committee to be such a success that they were determined to keep it as an annual affair.

More recently, and especially after Bath's fund-raising talents had been rewarded by the opportunity to host two matches against the visiting Australian Tourists in the 1970s, an annual Festival Dinner has become the main feature of the Festival Week. Bath is blessed with some magnificent venues for banquets and the historic Pump Room and the Guildhall Banqueting Room (where the dignified portrait of Frederick, Prince of Wales, surveys the diners) have both been used for memorable Cricket Week dinners. As a contrast to these grand locations, sell-outs at dinners held at the Bath Cricket Club on North Parade in the 1990s testify to the enduring appeal of the friendly atmosphere of this famous local club, many of whose players have represented Somerset.

From quiz nights (organised recently by Penny Lewis and Barry Clough) to river and canal cruises (the latter arranged in recent years by Michael Davis and Graham Ward), the local Bath Area Committee of Somerset County Cricket Club which runs the Festival, has organised fund-raising events to supplement the income of the Festival. For the Australia match in 1972, a sponsored walk was arranged and as evidence of the Committee's determination to raise money for the cause, Max Jeffrey, walking with the aid of crutches following a serious motor accident, completed two circuits of the Rec with Greg Chappell as his walking partner.

Every year a souvenir brochure is produced by the local Area Committee. It has a dual purpose; to provide an interesting memento of, and to raise funds for, the Festival. The Editor of the Somerset Wyverns Newsletter Edward Francis has regularly contributed an informative article to the brochure, the production of which in recent years has been in the hands of Robert Appleyard and Andrew Jackson, with Maurice Earle in charge of sales. The raffles run throughout the year by John Rhymer and the Grand Draw, organised by Barry Clough and Robert Appleyard, have also made significant contributions to the Committee's fund-raising efforts.

Since the mid-1990s, the Bath and North East Somerset Council, as part of its commitment to maintain the Somerset Cricket Festival for the city, has agreed to match pound for pound (currently up to a maximum of £7,000), the local committee's fund-raising efforts. In addition, the Council has generously agreed to waive charges for ground preparation and refuse collection. The negotiation, together with Somerset Chief Executive Peter Anderson, of this agreement with the Council

Frederick, Prince of Wales; oil painting by Jeremiah Davison, c.1741.

was a major achievement of Peter Yeman during his tenure of office as chairman of the local Area Committee during much of the 1990s.

Together with this financial support from the local Council, the sponsorship offered over a number of years by the Bath Spa Hotel has been of considerable assistance. In addition to a financial contribution towards expenses, the Bath Spa Hotel provides a top prize for the Grand Draw as well as making a presentation to the Somerset player of the Festival, an award won in 1999 by Rob Turner and in 2000 by Andrew Caddick.

For the past few years the Bath Area has sponsored the Somerset Under 16 team as part of a programme to foster the development of youth cricket in this country. As well as contributing towards the expenses of the team, the sponsorship involves support at matches and the award of a trophy to the nominated young cricketer of the season. As part of its mission to enable the people of North Somerset and Wiltshire to see first-class county cricket, the Bath Area Committee has always encouraged the attendance of local schoolchildren at the Festival. Nowadays, such a visit provides an opportunity to introduce the game to many in schools where cricket is no longer played. During the match against Kent in the 2000 Festival, over one hundred children from three schools attended play on the second day.

Years earlier, however, the annual visit of schoolchildren had an additional purpose. Ted Lewis remembered attending the Festival in the late 1920s when he was a pupil at St. Christopher's (now part of King Edward's School), and they all hoped to see former pupils Jack MacBryan and S.G.U. Considine score lots of runs. In those days, all the children had to sit on the grass around the perimeter of the playing field and concentrate hard on the cricket. They were taught to score, to record all the statistics in their books and the compilation of runs scored by batsmen and conceded by bowlers was treated as part of their mathematics syllabus for that term. They were also taught the etiquette of watching cricket and were never allowed to move during the course of an over, a discipline which, sadly, is all too frequently neglected by spectators today.

Twenty years later, Bath headmaster Fred Castle, on one of his all too rare appearances for Somerset at the Rec, was captaining the County in the absence of all three of Somerset's joint captains for that year (1948). Castle's aggressive batting delighted not only his pupils, seated around the boundary, but all local spectators and with Harold Gimblett's century and some fine bowling from Tremlett, Hazell and Wellard, was instrumental in securing a win for Somerset over Nottinghamshire by an innings. Given the extent of local loyalty, it is probable that some of those who were present as school-children in 1948 will have been among the numbers attending at the Festival in 2000.

CHAPTER 4

Four Memorable Somerset Victories

In the folklore of Somerset cricket in Bath, certain victories will always be remembered and two that have undeniable claims in this respect are the defeat of Surrey in 1920, 'as gratifying as it was unexpected', to use the words of Wisden, and the victory over the Australians in 1977; both of these are covered elsewhere herein.

A strong case could also be made for including the first ever Somerset win at the Rec, against Hampshire in 1900, when Tyler scored 51 and captured 13 wickets for 135. The trio of victories in 1946, against Kent (with Leslie Ames and Godfrey Evans in their team), Cambridge University and Hampshire, might well merit inclusion, as also the victory against Derbyshire in June 1970 when, set 252 to win in three hours and fifty minutes, Somerset achieved the target having three wickets in hand and with one ball to spare, Roy Virgin's 103 being the major innings in a fine all-round team effort. Spectators at more recent Somerset matches in Bath would argue probably for the inclusion of the defeats of Lancashire in 1985 and Surrey in 1994, including those outstanding individual performances from Victor Marks and Mark Lathwell respectively, but again these are referred to in a later chapter.

Judgement in these situations is inevitably subjective, but there are four matches, two of which were played against counties which eventually became County Champions, which merit serious consideration wherever memorable Somerset victories at the Rec are discussed. The first of these was in 1901 when Lancashire paid their first visit to Bath; they came without A.C.MacLaren, but still had England Test Players Johnny Tyldesley and Arthur Mold in their side. A magnificent opening partnership of 225 scored in two and a half hours between Lionel Palairet and Len Braund (82) provided the platform for Somerset to reach 412 for 5 by the end of the first day. Palairet, who was missed in the slips when 20, went on to score 182, including twenty two fours, and when he was eventually out, the score stood at 298 after only three and one quarter hours play. Palairet's innings of 182 remained the highest individual Somerset score at Bath until overtaken by Tom Young's 198 in 1924. The other major contributor for Somerset that day was Lewis with an innings of 68.

On the morning of the second day, some splendid hitting particularly by Mr. Vernon Hill (86) enabled Somerset to add a further 149 runs in just over one hundred minutes, the final total being 561. In reply, Lancashire scored 245 in just under 70 overs; a curious feature of the Lancashire innings was that all of the first nine batsmen made double-figure scores, the highest being 42 and the lowest 14. Of the Somerset bowlers, Cranfield returned the best figures of 5 for 69, the remaining wickets being shared by Gill, Woods and Braund. Before the close of play on the second day, Lancashire were being asked to follow on, and fast bowler Arthur Mold, somewhat uncharacteristically opening the innings with Mr. H.G.Garnett, was bowled by Gill for nought.

Lancashire thus found themselves, at the beginning of the third day, still more than three hundred runs behind Somerset. To save the match, therefore, a measure of caution might be considered correct, but Garnett (57) and Tyldesley (40) had other ideas. They put on 77 runs in three quarters of an hour, but after they were dismissed, both caught off the bowling of Braund, the batting collapsed and despite a spirited innings from Sharp (40), Lancashire were dismissed for 199, leaving Somerset as the victors by an innings and 117 runs. It was Len Braund with his leg-breaks who took most of the wickets in the Lancashire second innings, finishing with 6 for 51 but an outstanding feature of the match was the Somerset fielding, thirteen of the visitors' wickets falling to catches.

Lancashire finished third in the County Championship in 1901 and Somerset's memorable victory occurred three weeks before the greatest ever win in Somerset's County Championship history, the defeat at Headingley of Yorkshire, the only defeat suffered by Yorkshire in their Championship winning season of 1901.

Yorkshire were again striving for the County Championship when they came to the Rec in August 1959. They were without Trueman and Illingworth, playing for England against India at the Oval, and Somerset won the toss and elected to bat. The opening pair, Virgin and Lomax batted through 40 overs up to lunch and took the score to 73. Immediately after lunch, Virgin was dropped; he then went on to make his first 50 in county cricket and had made 68 when he was deceived by Wilson's flight of the ball and stumped. Lomax went on to make 92, McCool scored

*Lionel Palairet
returns to the
pavilion after
making 182
against
Lancashire.*

39 and Tremlett 30, but the most attractive batting of the day came after tea when Alley (56) and Greetham (49) both not out, added 103 in 65 minutes. Yorkshire's slow left arm bowler Don Wilson, who at one stage of the afternoon had taken 5 for 32, finished the day with 5 for 57.

Somerset declared at their overnight score of 342 for 5 and within a few overs, Yorkshire were 9 for 2 with both openers out. Taylor got an edge to a ball from Biddulph which sped to the boundary, but his relief at his good fortune subsided when McCool, fielding in the slips, pointed to the dislodged off bail. Close and Padgett counter-attacked with aggression and the score had advanced to 214 when Alley, who had just taken the new ball, bowled Padgett for 82. Close followed soon after having scored 128, and although their captain Ronnie Burnet tried to shore up the innings, Yorkshire declined to 275 all out. Somerset, with 46 for no wickets, extended their lead to 113 runs by the close of play.

After two days of sunshine, there was a change in the weather. Yorkshire continued to bowl through the drizzle and Somerset were all out for 187, Lomax (49), Virgin (37) and Alley (45) again making the top scores, with Close taking 6 for

Andrew Caddick and Ian Blackwell sign autographs at Bath, June 2000.

87 from his 33 overs. There was more rain at lunch-time but in the end, less than 15 minutes play was lost. Yorkshire thus required 255 to win in three and one quarter hours. At 55 for 2, Close joined Taylor and the score advanced by 78 in forty minutes. Close was then out for 34 (caught Stephenson bowled Langford), but only 103 were needed in 90 minutes with seven wickets left. Aided by some excellent wicket - keeping by Harold Stephenson, Brian Langford's bowling turned the tide. Despite some lusty hitting by Birkenshaw, the last seven Yorkshire wickets fell for 86 runs, and Somerset won by 16 runs, their first victory over Yorkshire for more than 50 years. Although Somerset won the match, Yorkshire eventually ended the season as County Champions.

In 1981 it was Nottinghamshire who won the County Championship. Before the title was safely secured, Nottinghamshire came to Bath in mid-June. The visitors, captained by South African all-rounder Clive Rice won the toss, chose to bat, and Todd (32), Randall (43) and Birch (63) took them to a total of 222. For Somerset, Colin Dredge had the best figures with 3 for 34 off 18 overs, but Garner, extracting lift from a slow-paced pitch, Moseley and Richards took two wickets each. When Somerset replied, Hadlee took an early wicket but Vivian Richards, first with Popplewell (47) took the score to 100 and then with Slocombe (50) doubled it to 208. The personal duel between Richards and Hadlee was a contest for the connoisseur. Hadlee beat the bat on a number of occasions and at one stage bowled a string of maidens to him; but Richards straight-drove the New Zealander for six and punished any ball slightly straying to the leg side. When Richards himself was out for 106, having hit two sixes and thirteen fours, Denning (39) and Marks (70) carried the score along briskly and Brian Rose was able to declare at 380 for 9. This declaration left just under one hour of the second evening for Nottinghamshire to bat. During that time, Garner and Moseley took the wickets of the first three batsmen in quick succession. On the last morning, only some brief resistance from Hadlee and Harris delayed the end, Garner finishing with 6 for 29 off 21 overs and Moseley with 2 for 39 off 15 overs. The margin of Somerset's victory was an innings and 61 runs.

As impressive as the margin of victory was the manner in which it was achieved. This was an outstanding all-round team effort by Somerset whose out-cricket was particularly memorable. The three most eye-catching moments came with Derek Taylor making a spectacular catch down the leg side to dismiss Clive Rice, who was aiming to hook Colin Dredge; and with two run outs, both achieved by Philip Slocombe with direct hits on the stumps from the covers.

The most recent match played on the Rec was Somerset's game against Kent in June 2000. This was the first match at Bath in the new structure of the County Championship, split into two divisions, with promotion and relegation between the two. On account of Somerset's excellent season in 1999, the County qualified for the higher Division One, and it was in this competition that the game against Kent was played. This was a match of fluctuating fortunes, an absorbing contest, in which first one side obtained a slight advantage, then the other, neither team being able to impose its will for any length of time.

On the first morning, the sun was shining and spectators, as they streamed into the ground, were asking who had won the toss. No announcement had been made, so Bath Area Committee Member, Michael Davis, an authoritative figure resplendent in his white jacket and sun-hat, went straight to the dressing-room to enquire of Kent captain Matthew Fleming. 'We're batting', said the surprised Fleming, 'is that all right?' Andrew Caddick, having returned to the Somerset team after Test Match duty with England, at once began to trouble the batsmen with his accuracy and the considerable lift which he obtained from the pitch. The only batsman who played him with assurance was Kent's overseas player and Indian Test Match batsman, Rahul Dravid whose fluent driving and ability to pick the right ball to hit took the score to 170, before he was caught for 90 by wicket-keeper Rob Turner down the leg side attempting to glance a ball from Graham Rose.

Matthew Fleming, together with Walker and Ealham, scored useful 20s and Kent were eventually dismissed for 261 off 81 overs, Caddick finishing with 6 for 57 off 25 overs, five of these dismissals falling to catches behind or close to the wicket. Somerset openers scored 47 without loss before the close but in the first over of the second morning, Marcus Trescothick was caught behind for 24. Batting almost throughout the second day, Somerset accumulated a total of 295 runs, mainly due to half-centuries from Jamie Cox (52), Piran Holloway (50) and Keith Parsons (62), together with 45 not out from Graham Rose. Three overs remained for Kent to bat and during that time Caddick dismissed opener Fulton for 4.

On the third day, Caddick and Steffan Jones bowled tightly, and before lunch Kent were 60 for 4. There then followed a stand of 99 between Walker (61) and Ealham (43) which put Kent firmly back in the game. With useful scores from wicket-keeper Paul Nixon (28 not out) and Fleming (23), Kent reached a total of 223, leaving Somerset 190 runs to win. For Somerset, Steffan Jones took 3 for 74 off 23 overs, to add to his two wickets in the Kent first innings, but it was the outstanding bowling of Andrew Caddick, with 4 for 40 off 25 overs, giving him match figures of 10 for 97 off 50 overs, that restricted the Kent total.

The pitch was taking spin and in left-arm off-spinner Min Patel, Kent had the bowler to exploit it; it was likely that to achieve a total of 190 Somerset would have to struggle and so it proved. Trescothick, whose successful season was later to be crowned with selection for England in both Test Matches and Limited Overs Internationals, was on this occasion out to the first ball of the innings. Although Cox and Holloway staged a partial recovery, taking the score to 41 before Holloway was stumped off Patel, another wicket fell before the close of play when the score stood at 50 for 3.

After three days of settled sunshine, there was rain early on the Friday morning, the fourth and last day of the match, although this did not delay the start of play. Skipper Jamie Cox was the man on whom Somerset hopes rested and he had appeared in confident form and taken the score to 68 when he was bowled round his legs by Patel for 43 The struggle intensified as Bowler (11), Parsons (18), Turner (17) and Rose (18) all started to make runs but none could exceed 20.

The Kent bowlers were accurate and runs were scarce. Patel bowled from the North Parade end almost throughout the innings (36 overs, of which 20 were maidens) and received sterling support from Ealham and Masters. From 68 for 4, the

The scoreboard at the Rec recording Somerset's victory over Kent in June 2000.

score advanced slowly, with wickets falling regularly, to 97 for 6 and then 152 for 8, when Graham Rose, who was batting with a runner, was out. Thirty-eight runs were still required when Ian Blackwell was joined by Andrew Caddick, who promptly struck Masters for four. Caddick then hit Patel over mid-wicket for six, the shot of the match and the first really belligerent stroke played off Patel during the entire second innings. It took the score to 165, so a further 25 runs were still needed but amid mounting excitement, the atmosphere changed. As Somerset's self-belief returned, Kent felt the game slipping away from them, and Blackwell (27) and Caddick (21) saw Somerset safely home to victory, having put on 41 runs for the ninth wicket. Only those who were there know just how close Kent came to winning the match.

The game finished just before tea on the fourth day. This was County Cricket at its best, an absorbing contest played on a pitch that was rated excellent, in a Festival match, and vindicating those administrators who had argued for the introduction of four-day cricket. Deservedly, it was Andrew Caddick who won the Bath Spa / Louis Powell Trophy for the Somerset player of the Festival, presented to him by Somerset President Michael Hill.

27

CHAPTER 5

THE GOLDEN AGE

SOMERSET'S ADMISSION TO FIRST-CLASS COUNTY CRICKET STATUS in 1891 coincided with what has been described as the Golden Age of English cricket, the period of some twenty years up to the start of the First World War.

At the beginning of this period, W.G. Grace was still playing, and scoring centuries, and the era was dominated by the names of such legendary batsmen as R.E.Foster, C.B.Fry, F.S.Jackson, A.C.MacLaren, R.H.Spooner (all amateurs) Tom Hayward, Jack Hobbs and Frank Woolley, Wilfred Rhodes and George Hirst, the last three being all-rounders, and all of whom played against Somerset at Bath. Another who played at Bath (in 1902, on one of his rare appearances for Lancashire) was the man regarded as the greatest bowler in England, S.F.Barnes. In a Test Match career of 27 matches stretching from 1901 to 1914, Barnes took 187 wickets at an average of less than 17 runs a wicket. During that time, he made less than 50 appearances for Lancashire preferring to play in non first-class cricket for his home county of Staffordshire.

Although Somerset prospered initially in championship cricket, finishing third in 1892 and sixth in 1894, for most of the next twenty years the County finished nearer, and sometimes at, the foot of the table. They had their share of talented amateur batsmen, men such as Lionel Palairet, whose batting was described as graceful and stylish, Henry Martyn and Randall Johnson, but their appearances were too infrequent; furthermore, although the County had in Len Braund one of the most gifted all-rounders in the country, the overall playing strength of the County was too limited to offer a sustained challenge to the major cricket counties. Somerset captains for most of this period, Sammy Woods and John Daniell, often found it hard work to raise a team, exemplified by the fact that in seasons 1908 and 1910 the number of cricketers who represented the County, in seasons with no more than 20 matches, were 31 and 38 respectively.

Spectators at Bath during the Golden Age were fortunate to see some of the strongest cricket sides in the country playing against Somerset. In the 17 seasons between 1898 and 1914, Yorkshire paid five visits to Bath, Lancashire went there on ten occasions and Middlesex and Surrey came twice. In those 17 seasons, Somerset won only eight and lost 25 of their 50 county championship matches at the Rec; in addition, of two matches each against Australia and South Africa one was lost and one was drawn. Yet, as the 1909 edition of Wisden reported 'The matches at Bath were much better supported than those at Taunton. At Taunton, the ill-success of the eleven in recent years has had a disastrous effect'.

Although the County's lack of strength in depth was the major reason for these somewhat modest playing results, temperament also played a part. The philosophy of Sammy Woods, who was captain until 1906 appeared to be exemplified in a remark attributed to him that 'draws were only good for swimming', and certainly Woods' overwhelming desire to secure a win (or perhaps, a gambling instinct) saw him preside, as captain of the Gentlemen, over their defeat by the Players who scored over 500 runs in the fourth innings to win the annual fixture at Lord's in 1901.

The first victory achieved by Somerset at the Rec came in May 1900 when Hampshire were defeated by seven wickets. It was against Hampshire in a rain- affected match in 1898, when less than three hours play was possible, that the first and only hat-trick at Bath by a Somerset player was achieved, Ernie Robson being the successful bowler. Both Robson and Edwin Tyler took five wickets each in this Hampshire innings and for this feat, each was rewarded by the County with a sov-

Wilfred Rhodes. Studies for the painting 'Wilfred Rhodes in Action', by Ernest Moore.

29

ereign by way of talent money. Rain prevented any play on the first day of the sub-sequent (1900) match and on the second day, the Hampshire captain, having won the toss, unexpectedly chose to bat. His side were dismissed for 81 and as the pitch dried out Somerset scored 249, with Gill (54), Tyler (51) and Daniell (41) all contributing useful scores. Although Hampshire made 209 in their second innings, Somerset were left with only 42 runs to win which was achieved for the loss of three wickets. Tyler, the Somerset spin bowler, was the hero on this occasion finishing with match figures of 13 for 135 from 53 overs.

During these years prior to September 1914, Hampshire visited Bath to play Somerset on eleven occasions (including a visit in June 1903 when the match was abandoned without a ball being bowled). Hampshire won three and Somerset three, including the victory in 1911, Somerset's solitary win in two seasons. This success was in large measure attributable to the all-round skill of A.E.Lewis, whose two innings of 93 and 20 were as important, in a low scoring match (the four completed innings produced a total of only 495 runs), as his match figures of 10 for 58.

Apart from the outstanding victory against Lancashire in 1901, noted in Chapter 4, the most satisfying achievements were the three consecutive wins against Gloucestershire in 1903, 1904 and 1905, the last being won by dismissing their opponents for 78 after Somerset had followed on. The professional bowlers, Cranfield, Braund, Robson and Lewis contributed significantly to these wins, Gloucestershire scoring only just over 1000 runs in six completed innings. Somerset's pleasure was all the more intense as Gloucestershire had triumphed in the first two encounters at Bath, in 1900 and 1902. The trio of victories had started in 1903 when Ernest Robson took 6 for 54 in Gloucestershire's first innings. Robson, whose career lasted almost thirty years up to 1923 is the Somerset player with the most appearances at Bath (64) and his 12 wickets in 1909 almost enabled Somerset to secure an unexpected win over Australia. He was supported, during the early 1900s, by Beaumont Cranfield, a slow left-arm spinner from Bath who claimed over 550 wickets during his 12 year career for Somerset and who, with match figures of 9 for 122, was primarily responsible for the defeat of Gloucestershire in 1904.

Two further matches were played against Gloucestershire during this period, both ending as draws, but the match in 1908 deserves fuller mention. Gloucestershire arrived at Bath on 11 June, the anniversary of their match the previous year at Gloucester when Northamptonshire were dismissed for 12 runs, still the lowest recorded total in county cricket. Both George Dennett, a slow left-arm bowler who took 15 for 21 in 21 overs in that match and Gilbert Jessop, who top-scored (with 22

Somerset v Gloucestershire, 1903. The photographs show, left to right, Lionel Palairet and Henry Martyn; Gilbert Jessop, after scoring 81; and A.E. 'Ted' Lewis.

and 24) in both Gloucester innings, were in their team which came to the Rec for the match. Although Dennett bowled 78 overs and finished with match figures of 6 for 144, it was Gloucestershire captain, Gilbert Jessop who dominated proceedings at Bath. He scored 143 out of 179 in only one and a half hours, hitting one six and 24 fours. As if this were not enough, Jessop scored 133 not out (including 25 fours) in the second innings; despite all these heroics, however, the Gloucestershire captain had to be content, as was the case the previous year against Northamptonshire, with a draw Somerset finishing the match still needing 103 to win with five wickets left.

While Jessop's achievement might be regarded as one of the batting high-lights of the Golden Age, the most admirable all-round performance at the Rec during these years was by George Herbert Hirst in Yorkshire's crushing victory by 389 runs in August 1906. On the field for almost the entire match, Hirst scored a century (111) in the first innings; he then bowled 26 overs taking 6 for 70 as Somerset replied with 125. Not enforcing the follow on, Yorkshire batted a second time with Hirst (117 not out) and Rhodes (115 not out) each scoring centuries. In Somerset's second innings, as a demoralised side set out to make 524 to win, Hirst bowled a further 15 overs taking 5 for 45. It was a sweet revenge for the man who, when Somerset were compiling 630 in their second innings at Leeds in 1901, had laboured for 37 overs costing 187 runs. On that earlier occasion, Hirst had confided to Sammy Woods that 'My feet are so sore I can hardly run up to the wicket'.

As this period drew to a close, following the declaration of war, the brightest hope for the future of Somerset cricket lay in the emergence of a young slow bowler, J.C. 'Farmer' White. He made his debut for Somerset at Bath in the match against Lancashire which provided one of the most exciting games of this era. White's contribution was modest but he did take one wicket. This match almost provided John Daniell with his finest hour, his 121 not out dominating the Somerset first innings. In the end, it was Lancashire's amateur fast bowler Walter Brearley, who bowled 63 overs in the match and took 11 wickets, who was just too good for the Somerset batsmen and Lancashire won by nine runs.

In four appearances at the Rec between 1903 and 1908, Brearley captured 32 wickets, Lancashire winning three matches with one ending in a draw. Wilfred Rhodes was another bowler who must have enjoyed his visits to the Rec. Rhodes, who continued playing until 1930, came to Bath on five occasions between 1898 and 1914, bowled in four of those matches and took 28 wickets at an average of just over 10 runs a wicket; for good measure, he also scored a century in 1906. Four of these five visits resulted in victories for the White Rose county, all by substantial margins; the remaining match ended in a draw.

CHAPTER 6

Four Impressive Personal Achievements

In the very first County Championship match played at the Rec, in May 1898, Somerset entertained Yorkshire, the strongest possible opposition. For that match, Yorkshire selected for the first time in a Championship game, a young, slow left-arm bowler named Wilfred Rhodes. Yorkshire were seeking to introduce a new talent to replace their international bowlers, Peate and Peel, whose careers had been terminated prematurely as a result of disagreements with Lord Hawke. Just twenty years of age, Rhodes was accordingly drafted into the side for the match at Bath. No more inspired choice could have been made, for Rhodes proved to be the discovery of the season.

Introduced into the bowling attack when Somerset were 42 for 2 in reply to Yorkshire's first innings score of 163, Rhodes proceeded with guile and cunning to deceive batsman after batsman, who were unable to read which way the ball would break. Three batsmen were clean bowled and after 13.4 overs, four of which were maidens, Rhodes finished off the Somerset innings with seven wickets for 24 runs. Both the Yorkshire and the Somerset first innings were completed on the first day (Monday) and on the Tuesday Yorkshire had made just over one hundred runs when the rain descended and eventually play was abandoned for the day. Half an inch of rain fell before a resumption could be made at noon on the third day. Quick runs were called for and at 174 Yorkshire declared leaving Somerset 234 to win.

Whereas in the first innings Lord Hawke had chosen two fast bowlers to open the bowling, in the second innings, with the sun drying the damp pitch, he asked Rhodes to start the attack together with fast bowler Schofield Haigh. In 25 overs, Somerset were all out, dismissed for 35, still the lowest score ever recorded at the Rec. Somerset were in some disarray, having suffered in the field; Newton had damaged his thumb and was unable either to keep wicket or to bat in the second innings; Tyler had split a finger and, although he batted, he was clearly in some discomfort. Even so, the innings represented a triumph for Rhodes who with his easy, natural action dismissed six batsmen for 21 runs. His match analysis of 26.4 – 10 – 45 – 13, is testimony to bowling of the highest class, assisted by outstanding wicket-keeping by David Hunter, who shared in six dismissals. At the end of the innings, the umpire presented the ball to Rhodes with the remark 'You've bowled well, young'un; perhaps you would like to have it mounted'.

Rhodes developed into one of the finest all-rounders ever to represent England, for whom he played in 58 Test Matches. He finished playing for Yorkshire in 1930, and throughout his career scored nearly 40,000 runs and took over 4,000 wickets. He appeared for Yorkshire at the Rec five times before 1914, and he was there again in 1927 and 1930, in this latter game, at the age of 53, having match figures of 7 for 54 off 34 overs.

Jack Hobbs(right) and Andrew Sandham open the Surrey innings at Bath.

A contemporary of Wilfred Rhodes, and on numerous occasions not only his colleague but his opening batsman partner in the England team, Jack Hobbs was much less successful on his visits to the Rec. His first five innings there for Surrey yielded only 51 runs, but in 1922 his scores were higher when he notched a 30 and a 60. In the following year, in search of his hundredth hundred, Hobbs was brilliantly caught by John Daniell for 0 in the first innings. Before the end of the day, he was batting again, and on the third day, Tuesday 8 May 1923, after batting for just over three hours, his century was achieved, his first ever against Somerset. Some nerves were undoubtedly evident during the early stages of Hobbs' second innings. Three of his partners were run out, one of them, Shepherd, to a brilliant piece of fielding by Considine. Indeed, there might have been a fourth; in the words of *The Times* 'with Mr Fender in, Hobbs started for a run which his captain would not have and must have been out if Mr MacBryan had not blundered'. After these early alarms, and with the help of some vigorous hitting by Bill Hitch, Hobbs began to play with more of his customary fluency and assurance. He hit J.C.White for a six and two fours to move into the nineties, but from 94 onwards, his runs came in singles until at 98, (in the words of the Bath Herald), 'a wild overthrow and a tarried return by Johnson sent up the century and Hobbs received an ovation'.

Despite those anxious moments in the 'nervous nineties', Hobbs' second fifty runs, to reach his century, were scored in 65 minutes, for the most part in masterly fashion. He had reached 116 not out, comprising two sixes and eleven fours when Fender declared. As news of Hobbs' achievement spread, messengers bringing telegraphed congratulations were constantly appearing at the match, some telegrams being even brought to him on the pitch!

Correspondents noted that Hobbs had followed in the footsteps of W.G.Grace who had achieved his hundredth hundred against Somerset (albeit at Bristol). Another interesting coincidence is that when Hobbs scored his hundredth run at Bath, he was partnered at the wicket by Harry Harrison, a Surrey batsman coming to the end of his 15 year career with the county. Harrison thus claimed a rare distinction, for at the Oval some ten years earlier, he had partnered Tom Hayward when Tom achieved his one hundredth hundred, scored against Lancashire in June 1913.

By the end of his career, Hobbs had scored 197 centuries, a record which still stands. Wilfred Rhodes said that Jack Hobbs 'was the greatest batsman of my time' and he seems to have been revered by all not only as a cricketer but for his personal qualities as a man. In the year 2000, Hobbs was chosen by Wisden as one of its five

'Cricketers of the Century' and, significantly, he was the only Englishman among the five.

There was no doubt that for the first half of the last century, slow bowlers were helped by the wickets being uncovered. By the time that Victor Marks began to play for Somerset, wickets were required to be covered, medium pace bowling was dominating county cricket, and the slow spin bowler generally had infrequent opportunities to shine. This did not, however, deter Marks who was Somerset's leading wicket taker for seven consecutive seasons in the 1980s. There was one particular occasion at Bath which the off-spinner would recall with pleasure. Curiously, it was in 1985, that season of limited success, when Somerset, with only one win and 16 draws in 24 matches, finished at the foot of the Championship Table; but the one win was at Bath and it was a victory to savour.

Somerset were playing Lancashire at the Rec and Victor Marks, acting as captain in the absence of Ian Botham who was playing for England at Headingley in the Test Match, won an important toss. Heavy overnight rain had prevented any play before lunch but Marks decided that Somerset should bat first. Before lunch on the second day, Somerset declared at 304 for 7 (Vivian Richards being top-scorer with 65). By the close, Lancashire had been dismissed for 153, Joel Garner taking 4 for 18 and Marks himself, with 30 overs of spin, taking 3 for 56. Lancashire were asked to follow on and during the third morning Marks began their downfall. In his first over, he had Folley caught off bat and pad at short leg. There then followed an interruption on account of the sun (see Chapter 18), and the minimum number of overs was reduced by eight. When play resumed, Marks clean bowled Fowler and O'Shaughnessy. Fairbrother, too, was bowled and in the same over, Abrahams fell to a catch. Three more wickets fell to Marks (all caught) and he took a catch to dismiss Jack Simmons off the bowling of Booth. Lancashire were all out for 89 and Somerset achieved their first and only County Championship win of the season. Marks had bowled with skill and accuracy and his figures of 8 for 17 in 22 overs, of which 15 were maidens, were the best of his career. Modest as always, he was reported in the Bath Chronicle as saying that 'it was a very good pitch to bowl on. In those conditions, all you have to do is to keep bowling line and length'. Lancashire captain John Abrahams was generous in defeat. While conceding that losing the toss was a disadvantage, he insisted that 'a lot of the credit must go to Vic who bowled superbly'.

The fourth impressive personal achievement to be recorded in this Chapter came in 1994, less than two weeks after West Indian batsman Brian Lara had made the highest individual batting total of 501 not out for Warwickshire against Durham

Mark Lathwell batting at Bath.

at Edgbaston. A large crowd had assembled at the Rec for the first morning of the match against Surrey, and having won the toss Somerset chose to bat. The innings was opened by Mark Lathwell and Marcus Trescothick and the score had reached 103 when the latter was out. Lathwell had scored his maiden century in first-class cricket against Surrey at Bath two years earlier; Trescothick was to score his maiden first-class hundred in the second innings of this match. Both of them were in due course selected to open the batting for England in Test Matches.

After three wickets had fallen for 156, Lathwell was joined by his captain, Andy Hayhurst; and together they added 216. With exquisite timing, Mark Lathwell compiled a superb double-century, the first by a Somerset batsman at Bath. In the process, he overtook Tom Young's score of 198, a record which had stood for 70 years. Lathwell's sparkling cover drives were interspersed with delicate late cuts and powerful pull shots and his innings included 33 fours. Even when the batsman is wearing the now obligatory (but aesthetically displeasing) helmet, there can still be artistry in the grace of a sweetly timed cover drive and Lathwell's innings produced many such eye-catching delights. He was out shortly before the close of play, having scored 206, an unforgettable innings for those privileged to be present in Bath that day, and one which also laid the foundation for Somerset's eventual victory.

CHAPTER 7

AMATEURS, PROFESSIONALS AND BENEFITS

BEFORE THE 1950s, it was a truth universally acknowledged in England that only an amateur, someone of independent means who played cricket otherwise than for money, had the necessary leadership qualities to captain a cricket side. The first professional cricketer to lead England in a home Test Match was Len Hutton in 1953. Somerset's first professional captain was Maurice Tremlett whose appointment took effect in 1956.

The distinction between amateur and professional was removed with the abolition of amateur status in the early 1960s, all being thereafter called 'cricketers'. Before then, on some grounds in England, amateurs and professionals would take to the field from separate entrances in the pavilion. Bath Cricket Club President John Ruddick recalled that at the Rec, the custom was for the amateurs to enter the field of play first, followed by the professionals. This was a custom which had mortified Jack MacBryan when, on his first appearance for the County (against Lancashire in 1911), he found that Len Braund was waiting for MacBryan to precede him out of the pavilion. The last Gentlemen v Players fixture was played at Lord's in 1962, but before then the realities of life in post-war Britain had caused the distinction to be blurred, although amateurs continued to represent Somerset throughout the immediate post-war period.

Up to 1939, however, all Somerset sides regularly contained many amateurs; often, they would number half a dozen and sometimes many more. This was not simply for the financial reason that amateurs did not have to be paid; it also reflected a deeply held belief that playing cricket was supposed to be fun and that what was perceived to be the spirit of the game was best maintained by amateurs. It was, of course, always the case that the side would contain some professional players, but whereas Somerset might field three or four, other sides, particularly from the northern counties, while still captained by an amateur, would be more likely to contain eight or nine professionals. Indeed in 1909 Wisden recognised that the achievement of Lord Hawke's great reign as captain of Yorkshire for over 25 years (1882-1908, during which Yorkshire won the County Championship eight times), lay in his 'unique work in managing for such a length of time a team composed almost entirely of professional players'.

Since organised cricket began in England well over one hundred years ago, it has been customary for a county to reward a long-serving professional player with a benefit match towards the end of his career. The beneficiary would be allowed to

Len Braund returns to the pavilion after another fine innings at Bath.

select a match, the gate receipts and collections from which he would be entitled to keep, subject to the deduction of certain match expenses. Over a period of nearly fifty years (1908-1953), three professional cricketers who between them provided years of stalwart service to Somerset and pleasure to spectators on the Rec, each chose a match at Bath for his benefit.

The first of these was Len Braund, an all-rounder who had joined from Surrey and who played regularly for Somerset (when not on duty for England for whom he played more than 20 Test Matches) in the early 1900s and ended his career only in 1920. Braund had played in the first Test Match ever staged at Edgbaston, against Australia in 1902, for the England team led by A.C.MacLaren, generally considered to be the strongest batting side ever to represent England, all eleven players having scored centuries in first-class cricket. Braund had been coached by W.G.Grace and attributed his improvement as a batsman largely to the instruction he received from the famous Doctor.

Braund chose for his benefit Somerset's fourth match at Bath that season, played against Surrey at the end of August 1908. Somerset had selected their best eleven, a team captained by Mr J.Daniell which comprised eight amateurs, including Mr Henry Martyn that most talented wicket-keeper batsman who, after his retirement two years earlier, returned to first-class cricket specifically for this game, but neither he nor his colleagues had much chance to shine. Some play was possible on the afternoon of the first day (Thursday) and Surrey, having lost both Hobbs and Hayward for single-figure scores, reached 180 for 7 thanks largely to an undefeated stand of 72 between Davis and his captain Mr. H.D.G. Leveson-Gower, who was later in his life (1930) awarded the freedom of the Borough of Scarborough for his services to cricket, especially festival cricket.

Rain on the Thursday night and again on the Friday prevented any further play despite some herculean efforts to dry the pitch. The Bath Chronicle reported that these included the obtaining of blankets from Braund's home which, in intervals of sunshine, 'were spread over the pitch and the light roller used to squeeze the water into them; when saturated, they were wrung out and applied again'. Coupled with a drying wind on Friday night, this procedure was so successful that play would have started on time on Saturday but for another storm which hit the city around mid-morning causing the captains to decide to abandon the match as a draw.

The Bath Chronicle later summed up the match in these terms: 'Last week another county cricket match was ruined by rain and it was all the more regrettable that there were only three hours play instead of three days'. The newspaper informed its readers that 1700 paying spectators had attended on the first day and assured them that the monetary results of the match from Braund's point of view would not be so barren as many had been led to expect because the Somerset Treasurer Mr. Gerald Fowler had insured the gate. In addition, benefit subscription lists had opened earlier in the season and Braund, who had twice visited Australia with Test Teams led by A.C.MacLaren and P.F.Warner, found that the citizens of Australia had contributed 16 guineas towards his benefit fund, five guineas being sent by the Melbourne Club. When Len Braund was offered another benefit after the First World War, however, he thanked the Committee respectfully, but declined.

Some 22 years later Tom Young, who was born in Bath and who had started playing for Somerset in 1911, selected for his benefit the match against Sussex at the end of July 1930. Never in the best of health following damage to his lungs suffered in the First World War, Tom Young nevertheless played over three hundred matches for Somerset scoring more than 13,000 runs and taking over 400 wickets. He had made his personal best total in Somerset's highest ever score of 675 for 9 declared, achieved against Hampshire at Bath in 1924, an occasion when the Somerset side included nine amateurs. Bath Area Committee Member Jack Endacott recalled being told by his father that Tom Young used a new bat for this match and, having scored 198, decided never to use it again but to keep it as a souvenir! It was also said that if personal scores had been recorded on the scoreboard that day, Tom would have ensured that he reached his 200. The deficiencies of the scoreboard then in use at the Rec were noted with shame by more than one Bath resident.

Each day of the benefit match against Sussex was affected by rain, with no cricket at all on the last day. In between the showers, Somerset made 138 and Tom Young, opening the batting, contributed 11. Sussex were then dismissed for 99, with J.C.White taking 7 for 47 off 20 overs, and Somerset made a few runs at the start of their second innings. Wisden recorded that 'the takings from the gate did not reach £100 [but it] was gratifying to learn later in the year that although the match itself produced so little money, efforts to make the benefit worthy of the great services rendered to the county by Young were attended with so much success that in the end the sum realised amounted to nearly £750'. Following his retirement from first-class cricket in 1933 Tom Young, like Len Braund before him, became a first-class umpire. Sadly, ill-health forced him to abandon this second career and Tom died in Bath in 1936 at the early age of 45.

When Bertie Buse, who made his debut for Somerset in 1929, was awarded

41

his benefit in 1953, he chose the first match of the Bath Festival, with Lancashire as the visitors, starting on Saturday 6 June. This match was not affected by rain, but it was completed inside one day, a newly laid pitch, causing the ball to bounce unpredictably, being to blame. Cyril Washbrook, the Lancashire captain, was reported to be horrified when he saw the wicket and asserted that Lancashire would have refused to play if it had not been a benefit match. Lancashire had the resources to exploit the pitch to the fullest advantage and their England off-spinner, Roy Tattersall finished the match with figures of 13 wickets for 69 runs off 24 overs. Somerset were dismissed for 55 and 79 runs, and although Bertie Buse himself took six wickets and was instrumental in restricting Lancashire to a score of 158, the visitors still won comfortably by an innings, the match ending at 5.34 p.m.

Buse was a popular and respected cricketer; John Arlott noted his 'precise manner and dignified step'. Len Hutton, the finest English batsman of the time, graciously acknowledged that he had never 'been able to master his bowling'. Although a large crowd attended on the Saturday, and Derek Brown remembered helping the stewards with the benefit collection on that day, a match completed within one day amounted to a financial disaster for the beneficiary and Buse's plight evoked much sympathy. His widow Elsa recalled being at home on that Saturday afternoon when around six o'clock Bertie and Harold Gimblett walked into the house with the words 'It's all over'. Contributions to his benefit fund came from around the country; in addition, the Somerset Committee waived the requirement for reimbursement of expenses and Bertie Buse ultimately finished with the sort of sum (over £2800) which he might have expected from a good three-day benefit match.

Part of the fascination of cricket, as of all sport, is the element of unpredictability; this was amply demonstrated when Bertie Buse returned a few days later to the Rec for Somerset's next game against Kent. On this occasion, although 18 wickets fell on the first day, the pitch held firm for sufficient time to enable Somerset in their second innings to score over 400 runs, with Bertie Buse and Harold Gimblett both making centuries. Somerset's win was secured by 17 year old Brian Langford, who in only his second game for the County bowled 80 overs and took 14 for 156.

Since the abolition of amateur status in the 1960s the benefit custom has continued for all cricketers, albeit in different form. For most seasons there will be a Somerset player who has been awarded a benefit but its success relies much more now on fund-raising efforts throughout the whole year. No longer is the beneficiary dependent upon a selected match and the attendant vagaries of fortune and the weather. Recent Somerset beneficiaries have included Graham Rose (1997), Andrew

SOMERSET   LANCASHIRE LOST BY INNS & 24 RUNS

Saturday, Monday & Tuesday, June 6th 8th, & 9th, 1953.

	SOMERSET	First Innings		Second Innings	
1	Gimblett, H.	run out	0	c Wharton b Tattersall	5
2	Lawrence, J.	c Ikin b Tattersall	8	c Wharton b Statham	0
3	Smith, R.	c Place b Tattersall	9	b Statham	0
4	Tremlett, M. F.	c Statham b Tattersall	4	b Statham	1
5	Buse, H. T.	c Grieves b Tattersall	5	c Grieves b Tattersall	3
†6	Stephenson, H.	c Marner b Tattersall	8	b Tattersall	14
*7	B. G. Brocklehurst	c Marner b Hilton	2	c Hilton b Tattersall	2
8	P. D. Deshon	c Edrich b Tattersall	0	c Whaton b Statham	9
9	S. S. Rogers	st. Parr b Hilton	7	c Grieves b Tattersall	0
10	J. Redman	c Place b Tattersall	1	not out	27
11	Langford, B.	not out	7	b Tattersall	8
		b2 l-b2 w n-b	4	b1 l-b9 w n-b	10
		Total	55	Total	79

Fall of the wickets
1-12	2-13	3-17	4-22	5-34	6-40	7-40	8-47	9-47	10-55
1-3	2-3	3-5	4-7	5-26	6-27	7-36	8-37	9-44	10-79

Bowling Analysis		First Innings						Second Innings					
		O.	M.	R.	W.	Wd.	N-b.	O.	M.	R.	W.	Wd.	N-b.
Statham		8	4	14				10	4	13	4		
Tattersall		12.4	4	25	7			11.3	2	44	6		
Hilton		5	1	12	2			2		12			

	LANCASHIRE	First Innings		Second Innings	
*1	Washbrook, C.	l-b-w b Buse	20		
2	Ikin, J.	c Tremlett b Buse	8		
3	Place, W.	l-b-w b Buse	11		
4	Edrich, G.	c Brocklehurst b Buse	2		
5	Grieves, K.	c Tremlett b Lawrence	2		
6	Wharton, A.	b Redman	21		
7	Marner, P.	b Redman	44		
8	Hilton. M.	b Buse	19		
†9	Parr, F.	not out	15		
10	Tattersall, R.	c Stephenson b Buse	2		
11	Statham, B.	c Tremlett b Langford	6		
		b4 l-b4 w n-b	8	b l-b w n-b	
		Total	158	Total	

Fall of the wickets
1-22	2-33	3-41	4-44	5-46	6-116	7-117	8-140	9-155	10-158
1-	2-	3-	4-	5-	6-	7-	8-	9-	10-

Bowling Analysis		First Innings						Second Innings					
		O.	M.	R.	W.	Wd.	N-b.	O.	M.	R.	W.	Wd.	N-b.
Buse		12.4	3	41	6								
Redman		6	1	32	2								
Smith		1		8									
Langford		3		18	1								
Lawrence		8	2	31	1								
Tremlett		2		20									

Scorers—T. Tout & M. Taylor.   Umpires—E. B-Carter & J. S. Buller.
Hours of Play—1st day—11.30-6.30   2nd day—11.30-6.30   3rd day—11—5 or 5.30
Lunch Interval—1.30 to 2.10.   Tea Interval—Subject to state of game.
Somerset won the toss.   *Captain.   †Wicket keeper.   P.T.O.

Scorecard for Bertie Buse's benefit match.

Caddick (1999) and Peter Bowler (2000). Graham Rose, who has done as much as any Somerset player in recent years to support the Bath Festival, especially with his attendance at many of the social events, emphasised its enduring appeal. Writing in 1997, he affirmed that the annual visit to the Recreation Ground was 'one of the most enjoyable aspects of my Somerset career' a comment echoed by Peter Bowler in his speech at the Festival Dinner of 2000.

CHAPTER 8

THE GREAT AUSTRALIAN CRICKET TRADITION

ALTHOUGH SIR DONALD BRADMAN NEVER PLAYED AT BATH, the city has over the years been fortunate to witness the skills of many talented Australian cricketers. In July 1905, Warwick Armstrong (who later captained the all-conquering Australia side of 1920-21) scored 303 not out, which remains the highest individual score ever recorded at the Rec. With a century from Monty Noble and Victor Trumper's 86, the Australians amassed 609 for 4 declared in their first match against Somerset there. The touring team did not, however, win the match as centuries from Braund and Martyn enabled Somerset, captained at that time by an eminent Australian exile, Sammy Woods, to secure a draw.

Four years later, the Australians were back in Bath staying at the Empire Hotel. This time, Armstrong, Noble (then captaining the side) and Trumper managed just 28 runs between them in two innings (with Warren Bardsley adding another 17) in a low scoring game against Somerset; the visitors were eventually indebted to Charlie Macartney and Syd Gregory for their two-wicket win. But whereas the 1905 Touring side was unsuccessful in the Test Series against England, the 1909 Australians, following the shock of their near defeat at the hands of Somerset, went straight from Bath to Lord's to win the second Test Match and ultimately take the Series 2-1.

Over 60 years elapsed before spectators at Bath were next able to see the Australian touring team in action there. In the meantime, three outstanding Australian players made their cricketing skills available to Somerset in the 25 years after the Second World War. Bill Alley served the County as an all-rounder with distinction during a career of over 300 matches for them. In 1964 he captained the team, in the absence of the injured Harold Stephenson, in all four Bath Festival matches, and among many outstanding performances at Bath, Alley's contribution with bat and ball to Somerset's innings victory over a Worcestershire side containing Tom Graveney and Basil D'Oliviera in 1965 will always rank high.

Another all-rounder from Sydney, Colin McCool, who was good enough to represent Australia in 14 Test Matches between 1946-50, joined Somerset in 1956 when he was over 40 years of age and played more than 180 county matches. As well as being the best slip fielder whom Len Creed ever saw, and a useful leg-break bowler, McCool's 149 (including 25 fours and one six) helped Somerset to an innings win against Leicestershire in June 1959.

Then in 1968, the 19 year old Greg Chappell came to Somerset to gain experience of English conditions. An elegant batsman with an upright stance, Chappell subsequently played for Australia in 87 Tests, scored a century on his debut, captained the team on many occasions and ended his Test Match career in 1987 with an average of over 53. Having played for Somerset at Bath in the disastrously wet festival of 1968, and again the following summer, with limited success as a batsman but recording some useful bowling figures, Greg Chappell appeared at the Rec next as a member of the visiting Australian team of 1972. Thanks to the efforts of local businessman Max Jeffrey in raising sufficient funds from corporate sponsorship to underwrite the costs of the fixture, the match at Bath, although affected by the rain and ending in a draw, was a success for Somerset financially and for Greg Chappell personally, as he scored a total of 115 runs in two innings without losing his wicket.

The experience of 1972 combined with Max Jeffrey's continuing ability to persuade companies to provide financial support enabled Bath to stage the game against the next Australian side to visit England. The match at the Rec in May 1977 against the Australian tourists, then captained by Greg Chappell, is one which all Somerset followers will long remember. With the Australian side containing seven members of the team which defeated England in Melbourne two months earlier in the Centenary Test Match, including players of the calibre of Doug Walters and Rodney Marsh, and despite centuries by both Chappell and David Hookes, it was Somerset who won by 7 wickets in the first over of the final hour. The win was attributable to a brilliant all-round team effort by Somerset (with particularly notable contributions from Brian Rose, Ian Botham, Graham Burgess, Vivian Richards, Philip Slocombe, and on his Somerset debut, Joel Garner), although the visitors' cause was not helped by fast bowler Jeff Thomson being no-balled by umpire Dickie Bird fifteen times in his initial seven overs. This was the first time ever that Somerset had defeated the Australians and during the three days it is esti-

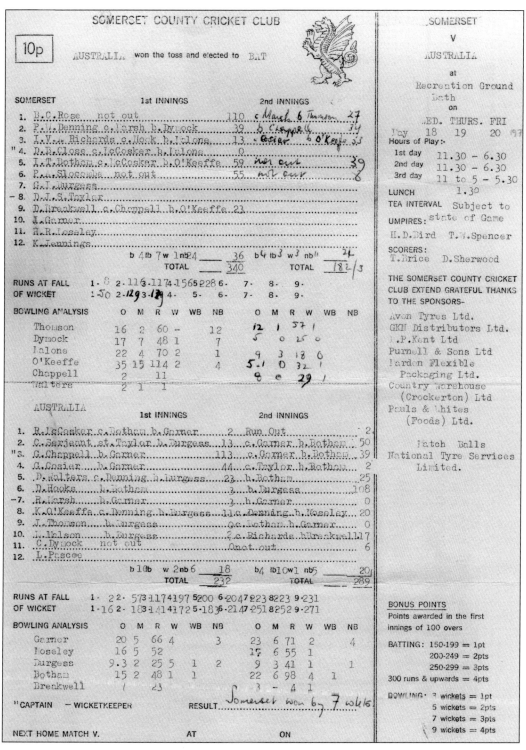

Scorecard of Somerset's historic victory over Australia, May 1977.

mated that over 15,000 spectators (including members) packed the ground. The match was also commemorated by the planting at the Rec, by the respective captains Greg Chappell and Brian Close, of two silver birch trees to the west of the pavilion.

Ian Botham bowling against Australia under the watchful eye of umpire H.D. 'Dickie' Bird, Bath, May 1977. Botham captured five wickets in the match.

Among the members of the defeated 1977 Australia team was Kerry O'Keeffe, a leg-spinner who represented Australia in over 20 Test Matches and who played nearly 50 matches for Somerset in 1971 and 1972. He found little help from the Bath pitch in 1977 and his 40 overs in that match yielded only 3 wickets for 144.

Ten years after that memorable victory, another young batsman from Sydney, Steve Waugh began to delight the Somerset crowds with his prolific scoring. In four innings during the Bath Festival of 1988, Waugh scored over 400

Captains Greg Chappell and Brian Close, assisted by Stan Hitt, plant a silver birch tree at the Rec in 1977.

runs including two centuries. As well as his run scoring ability, observers noted his self-belief and determination to succeed, characteristics which have enabled him recently (1999-2000) to lead Australia to one of the most successful twelve months of international cricket ever played. In the last 15 years, numerous Australian internationals have appeared at the Rec as overseas players with visiting counties. These have included Terry Alderman, who came to Bath with Kent, Stuart Law and Mark Waugh appearing there for Essex and Tom Moody playing for Worcestershire.

Somerset's own overseas player in 1996, Shane Lee from New South Wales, with 1300 championship runs at an average of 65, including a Somerset record-breaking seventh wicket stand of 278 with Rob Turner at Bath, was deservedly voted the County's player of that season; and Tasmanian-born Jamie Cox, who arrived in 1999 and immediately assumed the captaincy of the County side, led Somerset to its most successful season for years. He continued as captain in 2000 when the County succeeded in maintaining its first division status in both the County Championship and the National League. Cox's astute captaincy enabled Somerset to win both matches of the Bath Festival of that year; in addition, he scored Somerset's highest individual total of runs in the County's exciting two-wicket victory over Kent.

CHAPTER 9

More Overseas Cricketers

In addition to the four matches against Australia, Somerset have entertained at Bath teams from other Test Match playing nations. In the last one hundred years, South Africa have visited the city on three occasions, the West Indies twice and New Zealand and Pakistan once each. Star players from each of these countries have over the years displayed their skills at Bath for Somerset and other counties.

As one of the earliest Test playing nations, South Africa came to Bath twice in the years before the First World War, winning the first match by 358 runs and having the better of the draw in the second (rain-affected) match in 1912 when Somerset, having been set 270 to win, finished the match on 128 for 7. In this match, Somerset wicket-keeper Henry Chidgey was injured during the game and the South African captain A.D.Nourse graciously allowed him to be replaced. B.D.Hylton-Stewart, a bowler from Bath was accordingly drafted into the side with Mr B.L.Bisgood taking over the gloves. Having been dismissed in their first innings for 96, Greswell and Robson taking five wickets each, South Africa declared their second innings closed at 300 for 3, Nourse scoring a century. He was helped by S.J.Snooke who made 77 not out; Snooke clearly liked Bath for on his visit in 1907 he had made 157, the highest score of that game.

The third match against South Africa was played in July 1935, the tourists arriving in Bath fresh from their triumph in the second Test Match at Lord's. Their Vice-Captain H.B. Cameron, who was captain of the side in Bath, was hit on the head when attempting a big hit off Wellard; he had to be taken to hospital, and took no further part in the game. Somerset gained a first innings lead of 45 but, having bowled out the visitors in their second innings and needing only 240 to win, Somerset were dismissed for 188 and lost by 51 runs. The South African opening

The South African and Somerset teams at Bath, July 1935.

batsman, Bruce Mitchell, whose 164 not out in the Lord's Test Match made a major contribution to their win there, was not so successful with the bat in Bath scoring 21 in each innings. It was his clever spin bowling, however, which proved too much for Somerset on a wearing wicket, Mitchell ending the match with 5 for 45 off 22 overs. In this South Africa team and scoring 22 and 71 was A.D.Nourse, the son of their captain in 1912, and himself to become captain of South Africa at a later date. Frank Lee, with 86 and 32 runs and Arthur Wellard, with a match analysis of 8 for 153 off more than 50 overs, were the pick of the Somerset players. Although played in midweek, the game attracted a large number of spectators and match receipts totalled £650.

Bath's link with South African cricket continued with Bertie Buse who after retiring from the first-class game in 1953 went to South Africa for ten years and coached at King Edward VII School, Johannesburg. Among the pupils he taught there was Ali Bacher, South Africa's last Test captain before the years of isolation and more recently Chief Executive of the new United Cricket Board of South Africa. Bacher always remembered Buse's advice to him as a young batsman: 'Forward, boy, go forward!' which Bacher adapted to 'Forward, we are going forward' as the slogan for South African cricket in the 1990s.

51

Among many outstanding South African cricketers who have appeared in England since 1945, both Mike Proctor playing for Gloucestershire and Barry Richards playing for Hampshire produced excellent performances at Bath but Somerset followers will remember best of all the stylish batting of Jimmy Cook, the County's overseas player for three consecutive years ending in 1991. In those three seasons, Cook scored nearly 7000 runs in the county championship for Somerset, of which over 500 (including two centuries) were made at Bath at an average of nearly 64. Another for whom the city had immense appeal, Cook recalled how in his first match at Bath he had hoped that Somerset would be able to bat first; Kent however won the toss and ran up a score of over 500.

In the next match, Cook's wish was granted, Somerset choosing to bat first against Gloucestershire. By mid-afternoon, Somerset were all out for 73, Courtney Walsh taking 7 for 19 off 16 overs; Cook's contribution in the first innings was 12 but he fared much better in the second with 147. The mention of Courtney Walsh is a reminder of the substantial array of West Indian talent which spectators at Bath have been privileged to see. The exploits of Vivian Richards, Joel Garner and Hallam Moseley contributed hugely to Somerset's success in the 1970s and 1980s, and in the last 25 years many other great names in West Indian cricket – Clive Lloyd, Gordon Greenidge, Desmond Haynes and Curtly Ambrose among them – have appeared at the Rec. The outstanding performance was that 7 for 19 in 1989 for Gloucestershire of Courtney Walsh, the bowler who overtook first Richard Hadlee and then Kapil Dev to become in the year 2000 the highest wicket-taker in Test Matches, his total in March 2001 passing 500.

The West Indian touring team first appeared in Bath in 1928 when the match was drawn. Among those playing for the visitors on that occasion was C.V. Wight from Guyana, whose namesake Peter Wight, also from that country, was some 25 years later to begin an illustrious career for Somerset. England won all three matches of that 1928 Series, each one by an innings. When the West Indies next came to Bath in 1963, they were a much stronger side and in due course won the ensuing Test Series by three matches to one, with one drawn. They visited Bath at the end of May and although their much respected captain Frank Worrell scored only 12, a century by Basil Butcher and an exhilarating 112 from Garfield Sobers (he reached his hundred in 105 minutes hitting one six and nineteen fours) took the West Indies score to over 400 and enabled the visitors to win by an innings. Fast bowler Charlie Griffith had match figures of 7 for 35 off nearly 30 overs, Lance Gibbs took 6 for 98 off 44 overs, and Worrell himself, nearing the end of his career, bowled 51 overs in the

New Zealand cricketers visit Wookey Hole caves, June 1931.

match finishing with 4 for 79.

Of those New Zealanders who have recently graced the Test Match arena, Martin Crowe scored three centuries for Somerset at Bath in the 1980s. Earlier, Richard Hadlee, who during his career took over 400 Test Match wickets and who played a major part in Nottinghamshire winning the County Championship in 1981

53

appeared in Bath during that season. During the 1970s, Glen Turner made a century at the Rec for Worcestershire and Geoff Howarth scored a fifty for Surrey. Each of these two batsmen appeared in more than 40 Test Matches for New Zealand and captained their country.

Just before they played their first ever Test Match in England (at Lord's in 1931), New Zealand came to Bath for a game against Somerset. The match was evenly poised with Somerset 190 runs ahead with one wicket remaining when rain at lunchtime on the third day caused the match to be abandoned. The visitors were captained by Tom Lowry who a few years earlier, while a student at Cambridge University, had played for Somerset for three seasons on the basis of a 'qualification' which would not now bear too much scrutiny. Raymond Robertson-Glasgow, who played for both the Gentlemen and Somerset with him considered Lowry a remarkable cricketer with an ability to keep his colleagues amused with his entertaining comments on the run of play.

The Somerset XI for the first match played at the Rec, July 1897.

The Philadelphians, Somerset's first opponents at the Rec, July 1897.

The match in Bath started on a Saturday and as there was no Sunday play in those days, a visit to the well-known Somerset tourist attraction Wookey Hole was arranged. The excursion, which involved a descent into the caves followed by a crossing over their length, and then tea, was organised by Captain G.W.Hodgkinson, an amateur who had played a few times for Somerset in the days before the First World War, on one occasion opening the batting at Bath with Lionel Palairet.

Although Somerset's overseas player for five seasons in the 1990s Mushtaq Ahmed performed at Bath in five county matches during those years, taking ten for 116 in the victory over Sussex in 1995, and Intikhab Alam (Surrey) and Imran Khan (Sussex and Worcestershire) appeared at the Rec in the 1970s, the most outstanding performance by a Pakistani player there was by Zaheer Abbas, who in two innings in 1981 scored a total of 365 runs for Gloucestershire, without being dismissed. While discerning spectators will have appreciated Zaheer's dazzling strokeplay, the match was also likely to be remembered in Somerset on account of the rearguard action of Brian Rose and Peter Roebuck, both of whom suffered leg injuries while fielding, and who batted together for 45 minutes at the end of the third day to save the match.

The one visit of the Pakistan Touring team to Bath was in 1974. It was Ian Botham's first season for Somerset, his second match of the Bath Festival and he took a wicket with his first ball, having Shafiq Ahmed caught by Graham Burgess for 0. With a not out century from Mushtaq Mohammad (who had previously appeared in Bath for Northamptonshire) and a fine innings from Asif Iqbal, Pakistan declared and then dismissed Somerset, giving the visitors a lead of 96. On the final morning, Intikhab Alam, having hit five sixes in just over 20 minutes declared again, setting Somerset a target of 320 in five hours. Burgess (90), Taylor, Richards and Close all did well with the bat and when the last 20 overs began Somerset were 246 for 5. Although both Botham and Breakwell batted with spirit, the task was just too much for the home County and their valiant attempt failed by 5 runs.

India and Sri Lanka have never played at Bath but the man with the greatest number of centuries for India and scorer of more than ten thousand Test Match runs for his country Sunil Gavaskar played in Bath for Somerset during his one season with the County in 1980. He will be remembered in Bath particularly for his innings of 54 (including 5 sixes) which secured a win for Somerset in the limited overs match against Glamorgan that year; and during the Festival of 2000, spectators witnessed an innings of the highest class by India's Rahul Dravid for Kent.

Many years earlier, K.S.Duleepsinjhi playing for Cambridge dominated the first day's play when the University visited Bath in 1925. The following year, he appeared again at the Rec, this time scoring 60 runs in two innings for Sussex in a drawn game. Before that, Somerset had themselves welcomed two gentlemen from India into their side. Prince Narayan, son of the Maharajah of Cooch Behar, played only once at Bath scoring 3 and 16 in the match against the Australians in 1909. The other gentleman was M.P. 'Pyjamas' Bajana, who represented the County in some 50 matches and scored a century at Bath in Somerset's victory over Warwickshire in 1920.

During the 1985 Festival, there was a one-day match (not a first-class fixture) against Zimbabwe before they were accorded the status of a Test Match playing country; this resulted in a win for Zimbabwe, an innings of 42 from 19 year old Graeme Hick contributing to the visitors' victory.

The history of Somerset County Cricket on the Rec started with the visit of the Philadelphians from the United States in 1897. Since then, spectators at Bath have been fortunate to watch many teams from overseas playing against Somerset at the Rec as well as many international stars competing in county cricket matches there. While further visits to Bath from International Touring teams are unlikely to be made, the opportunity to watch individual overseas stars in county cricket should continue as long as the Festival itself.

CHAPTER 10

BETWEEN THE WARS

IN THE FIRST FEW SEASONS following the resumption of cricket after the Armistice, Somerset achieved higher positions in the County Championship than in those immediately prior to the First World War. In 1919, when championship matches were limited to two days, Somerset finished jointly with Lancashire in fifth position, and in the five subsequent seasons the County never fell below tenth place. From 1925 to 1929, however, the County ended the season in either fourteenth or fifteenth place.

Captained again by John Daniell, Somerset still featured more amateurs than most other counties, but for the first half of the 1920s, they appeared more regularly and with greater consistency. The highlight of the 1920 season, and probably of the whole decade, was the County's victory over Surrey at Bath. In that match, Somerset fielded ten amateurs and Len Braund (in his last season for the County). Somerset, having lost the toss, were invited to take first innings, and proceeding with due caution, they batted almost throughout the day to make 223, with P.R.Johnson (51), M.P.Bajana (40) and J.Daniell (36) making the highest scores. Keeping Jack Hobbs back for the following day, Surrey decided to open with wicket-keeper Herbert Strudwick (promoted from his usual position at number 10) and Andrew Sandham, who batted out the few remaining overs and the day closed with Surrey on 15 for no wicket.

By lunchtime on the following day, the Surrey total had advanced to 108, but in the process they had lost eight wickets. Some outstanding fielding (see Chapter 12) and bowling caused this upset and soon after lunch, Surrey were dismissed for 139. Somerset's lead of 84 was increased to 178 with an exhilarating opening stand between Johnson (45) and Sydney Rippon (55) and although a middle-order collapse ensued, Somerset's tail-enders scored sufficient runs to take the total to 194, thus setting the visitors a target of 279 runs. While Ducat (71), Fender (31) and Hitch (41) were batting, it looked as though Surrey might achieve an unlikely win but although their total of 246 was the highest innings of the match, the Somerset bowlers ultimately prevailed. While J.C.White bowled the most overs (57) for Somerset in this match and took 4 for 88, it was two other amateur bowlers Hardy and Bridges, with 14 wickets between them (nine of which were clean bowled) who secured the victory.

The supreme compliment to Somerset's amateur tradition came in 1924 when four of their cricketers were selected to play for the Gentlemen in the annual match against the Players at Lord's. Three of these were Jack MacBryan, a stylish right-hand batsman who had survived over three years as a prisoner of war of the Germans, M.D.Lyon, another attractive batsman, and Raymond Robertson-Glasgow, a fast bowler. The quartet was completed by an outstanding amateur bowler, J.C.White, one of the greatest players ever to represent Somerset.

It was also in 1924 that Somerset amassed their highest ever score in county cricket - 675 for 9 declared - overtaking their previous highest total of 630 scored at Leeds in 1901. The visitors to the Rec were Hampshire, and their captain, the Honourable Lionel Tennyson (grandson of the poet), having had the misfortune to be stung by a wasp on the lower lip while travelling by train to Bath, had the good luck to win the toss. At the end of the first day (Saturday), the Hampshire score stood at 368 for 5 and they added a further 85 runs on the Monday morning before being all out for 453, centuries being scored by two of their amateur batsmen, Day and Aird. For Somerset, the wickets were shared by Bridges (3 for 129), Critchley-Salmonson (2 for 97) and White (5 for 122), and between them, these three bowled 110 overs.

Faced with such a total Somerset might have succumbed; instead, inspired by a magnificent innings of 198 from Tom Young (scored in 3 hours 50 minutes and containing two sixes and 26 fours), they finished the day on 424 for 4. MacBryan made 45 and Sydney Rippon was 51 not out, but the excitement of the day was provided by the stand between Young and M.D.Lyon who put on 245 for the second wicket before Lyon was caught off Tennyson for 87. The Bath Chronicle reported Mr John Daniell as saying: 'I have never seen two finer hitting innings in the course of my experience'.

Rippon was out early on the Tuesday morning for 53 but White (62), Critchley- Salmonson (66 in 40 minutes) and Daniell (56 not out) maintained the momentum and a further 250 runs were added before Daniell declared the innings closed at 675 for 9, giving the home county a lead of 222. When Hampshire then lost their first two wickets for 17, Somerset must have scented victory, but although more than 50 overs were bowled and Daniell tried seven bowlers, Mead (70 not out) saw the visitors safely to 160 for 3 and the match was drawn.

The most accomplished of the amateur batsmen in the 1920s were Lyon, MacBryan and P.R.Johnson. Others who appeared with regularity were R.A.Ingle, later to captain the side in the 1930s and C.C.C.Case, both of whom played in more than 250 matches for the County during the period between the wars, with Case scoring two centuries at Bath during his eleven-year career. H.D.Burrough and E.F.Longrigg, the latter captaining the side in the last two seasons before the Second World War, each made over 150 appearances for the County. Throughout this period, Somerset continued to rely on infrequent appearances by other amateurs, including many of those mentioned in Chapter 11, men from Bath like Amor, Considine, Powell and R.P. Northway.

These amateurs were supported by a core of useful professionals, players like Tom Young, the Lee brothers, Frank and J.W., who opened the batting on numerous occasions, and from 1930 onwards, by Arthur Wellard; and throughout much of this period, there was playing for Somerset Wally Luckes, an

J.C. White batting at Bath.

accomplished wicket-keeper who scored the only century of his lengthy career against Kent at Bath in 1937.

The man who dominated Somerset cricket between the wars was J.C.White. As his career progressed, he developed into a useful batsman, and towards its end White was featuring more regularly in the top third of the Somerset batting averages. He scored six centuries for Somerset, one of which was achieved at Bath. It was however as a slow left-arm bowler, who relied more on flight and length than on spin, that J.C.White achieved fame. Coached by Edwin Tyler, White had before 1914 shown signs of his promise, but it was after 1918 that his talent was clearly revealed. In each of the fourteen seasons between 1919 and 1932, White took 100 wickets. He captained Somerset for five years, and represented England in 15 Tests, making a major contribution to the defeat of Australia at Adelaide in 1929, and captaining England against South Africa later that year.

Usually finding the pitch at Bath to his liking, White captured over 230 wickets (at an average of 15 runs a wicket) in the 35 matches in which he bowled for Somerset at Bath during those 14 seasons. In that time, he bowled nearly 2000 overs at the Rec, and if the match against Worcestershire in 1919 were included, when White's match figures were 16 for 83, his averages would be even more impressive. (This game was a first-class match but did not feature in the County Championship as Worcestershire did not enter the Competition that season).

Three Somerset victories at Bath, each one by an innings, exemplify the influence which White exerted over this period. In 1921, Essex were dismissed for 111 and 129, White's match figures reading 12 for 79 from 64 overs, half of which were maidens. Five years later, in Somerset's defeat of Derbyshire, the slow left-armer's haul of wickets in the match totalled 8 for 77 off 60 overs. Both of these performances were eclipsed six years later in the match against Glamorgan in 1932 when White, having taken 6 for 45 off 42 overs in the first innings, proceeded to destroy the Glamorgan batting with 9 for 51 from 28 overs in the second innings.

Until the arrival of Arthur Wellard in 1929, White was in most matches bowling with only modest support at the other end. Ernie Robson had retired in 1923 after a career of nearly 30 years; Bridges, Young and J.W.Lee all bowled tidily at times, as did W.T. Greswell on his rare appearances, but all too frequently it was on White that the burden of dismissing the opposition fell.

As White's career drew to a close (he relinquished the captaincy in 1931 and finally retired in 1937 at the age of 48), new stars were emerging to further the cause of Somerset cricket. There was Arthur Wellard, who began his first county champi-

S.G.U. Considine.

onship match for Somerset at the Rec in 1929, taking 4 for 99 against Worcestershire in a rain- affected match which ended as a draw. A fast bowler of genuine pace, he started to accumulate wickets during his appearances at Bath. This wicket-taking reached a climax in three seasons immediately before the Second World War. In 1936, 1937 and 1939, against Northamptonshire, Worcestershire, and Leicestershire respectively Wellard took 12, 11 and 9 wickets in the match, each one resulting in a win for Somerset. In the Bath Festival of 1938, Wellard was playing for England against Australia at Lord's.

Although originally selected for his bowling, Arthur Wellard will be remembered by many for his batting. He was loved by the crowds for his big hitting. In his Somerset career, he scored over 11,000 runs (at an average of nearly 20), and a large proportion of these runs came in sixes. Spectators at the Rec particularly enjoyed his innings of 70 against Northamptonshire in 1936, including six sixes and three fours.

It was in the mid-1930s that another much-loved Somerset batsman and famous big-hitter, Harold Gimblett started his county career. He delighted spectators at Bath for many years before and after the war, but his most memorable achievement at the Rec came in 1936 when the Northamptonshire bowlers were struck to all parts of the ground. In an innings of 143 scored in just over three hours, Gimblett hit seven sixes and seventeen fours. John Ruddick recalled seeing Harold Gimblett, in a match against Hampshire (just after the war), hit for six the first ball after lunch, bowled by Hampshire fast bowler O.W. 'Lofty' Herman, the ball landing in Johnstone Street!

Joining Somerset just after Wellard, with whom his name was always linked, was fast bowler Bill Andrews, who served Somerset as a player for nearly twenty years and thereafter acted as coach. He played little at the Rec before 1935 but once he had been re-engaged by Somerset in that year, his career blossomed. Andrews' finest performances at the Rec, when he took 9, 10 and 13 wickets respec-

The Somerset XI at the Bath Festival, June 1938. From left to right, back row: H. Hazell,
W.T. Luckes, W.H.R. Andrews, H.T.F. Buse, F.S. Lee, H. Gimblett.
Front row: L. StV. Powell, R.A. Ingle, E.F. Longrigg, M.D. Lyon, H.D. Burrough.

tively, came against Gloucestershire (1935), Kent (1937) and Middlesex (1939), each match resulting in a win for Somerset. Operating together, Andrews and Wellard were a formidable combination of fast bowlers.

Taking over the slow bowling role from J.C.White was Horace Hazell from Brislington. By the mid 1930s Hazell was playing regularly for the County and during his Somerset career, he took nearly one thousand wickets. He never had much luck as a bowler at the Rec before the war (he was much more successful in the late 1940s), but his stirring deeds as a number eleven batsman were long remembered.

Apart from his match-winning innings against Gloucestershire in 1935 (described in Chapter 12), Hazell's most memorable achievement was to hit Hedley Verity for twenty-eight in one over. This onslaught on England's greatest spin bowler of the 1930s comprised four sixes and one four, and provided the crowd with a few moments of excitement and cheer before Yorkshire duly completed their victory by an innings.

Although he was much more successful with the bat on this visit to Bath, scoring 89 in 1936, Verity was just one of the many England stars whom spectators at Bath were privileged to see during this period. Four years earlier, Verity had captured 9 for 41, and with Bowes taking 6 for 59, Yorkshire twice dismissed Somerset for under 100 runs. Walter Hammond played only once at Bath, scoring 53 in a rain-affected match, but his Gloucestershire and England colleague Charles Barnett played one of the finest innings ever seen at the Rec when he scored 194 (including eleven sixes) in 1934.

As well as those whose achievements have been recorded elsewhere in this book, other England players visiting Bath included Maurice Leyland and Herbert Sutcliffe, neither of whom troubled the scorers greatly when Yorkshire visited in 1936, although Sutcliffe had made some runs in Yorkshire's two-day victory in 1932; E.H. 'Patsy' Hendren (Middlesex), Philip Mead (Hampshire), Maurice Tate (Sussex) all performed well at the Rec and the Kent quartet of Percy Chapman, Leslie Ames, A.P.Freeman and Frank Woolley all made important contributions to their side's 8-wicket win in 1930.

The following year, when Nottinghamshire came to Bath, spectators had the opportunity to watch Larwood and Voce bowling, just eighteen months before they went to Australia with the MCC (England) team captained by D.R.Jardine. At Bath in 1931, the Notts fast bowling pair collected eleven wickets between them. In an interview given to the Bath Chronicle over 50 years later Bertie Buse, who started playing for Somerset as an amateur, turning professional only in the mid-1930s, remembered the match. He was just 20 years old and he had to face Larwood: 'I walked out to the wicket full of apprehension and took my guard. I saw a small stocky figure walking back towards the pavilion – I thought he was going to walk into the pavilion. There was a flurry of arms and legs; I didn't see the ball – and my stumps went flying. I was out for a duck. He was terribly fast'. At least Buse took a few wickets and in the second innings scored a few runs (he thought Larwood took compassion on him and bowled slower!), but Nottinghamshire won the match early on the third day.

Although the side was becoming more settled in the 1930s, with regular service from a loyal core of talented professionals, such as Andrews, Gimblett, Hazell, the Lee brothers, Luckes and Wellard, Somerset managed just three times in this decade to finish in seventh position, more often languishing in thirteenth place or lower in the Championship table. Results at Bath between the wars did, however, show an improvement on those of the years of the Golden Age. From 1919 to 1939, Somerset played 55 County Championship matches at the Rec; of these, 16 were won, 17 were lost and there were 22 drawn games. In addition, there was one match, against Essex in June 1924, which was abandoned without a ball being bowled. It must, however, be acknowledged that during these 21 seasons, when Yorkshire won the County Championship 12 times and Lancashire were 5 times winners, the White Rose county visited the Rec on only four occasions and Lancashire did not play there at all.

CHAPTER 11

Somerset Personalities from Bath

In addition to the communal activity of hosting Somerset matches at the Rec, individual Bath residents have made major contributions to the welfare of Somerset cricket both as players and as administrators. In the pavilion of the Bath Cricket Club in North Parade there is a photograph of the Club XI in 1933 which reveals that playing for Bath that year were nine players who represented Somerset at various times, some more frequently than others. These were Stanley Amor, an amateur wicketkeeper who captained the Bath Club from 1914-1950 and who appeared 26 times for Somerset over a 20 year period, E.F.Longrigg, Bertie Buse, Louis Powell, Ulick Considine, R.P.Northway, E.J.H.Hart, H.H.Humphries and R.A.Gerrard. All represented Somerset at the Rec except R.A.Gerrard, whose three appearances for the County were at other grounds. Others who played for Bath Cricket Club and for Somerset included Len Braund, Dickie Burrough, Fred Castle, E.P.Collings, the Rippon twins and Tom Young. Some of these, Considine, Hart, Longrigg and Young among them, also played for Lansdown, and from this famous local club there were many others who represented the County. Among these were the Bath solicitor Reggie Ingle, who captained Somerset from 1932-37, Leslie Angell, Frank and Jack Lee, Jack MacBryan and the Palairet brothers.

Jack MacBryan was an amateur, an elegant batsman who played his first game for Somerset against Lancashire at the Rec in 1911. It was in the 1920s, however, that he flourished at the wicket, and his form for Somerset earned him selection for the Gentlemen in both 1923 and 1924. Ironically, MacBryan always believed that the greatest compliment paid to him as a cricketer was a remark which he over-heard Wilfred Rhodes make to George Hirst: 'Jack plays more like a Yorkshire pro-fessional than a Somerset amateur'. In 1924, MacBryan achieved a distinction unique in English cricket. He was selected to play for England in the Fourth Test Match that year against South Africa at Old Trafford but torrential rain ended the match at 4 p.m. on the first day, when the South Africa total stood at 116 for 4, and there was no play on the remaining two days. MacBryan was not selected for anoth-er Test Match, so he became the only Test cricketer who played for his country, but who never batted, bowled or dismissed anyone in the field.

Both L.C.H. and R.C.N. Palairet later held office as President/Chairman of Somerset County Cricket Club, but the Bath figure who dominated Somerset crick-et for a period of some forty years was John Daniell. A gentleman of independent means, Daniell captained the side for a total of thirteen seasons, both before and after the First World War and later acted first as Secretary of the County and then, immediately after the Second World War, as its President and Chairman. Daniell is

Somerset Chairman E.F. Longrigg (right) with Club President Lord Hylton, 1966.

remembered for fielding in his Homburg hat, some brilliant close to the wicket catches, and his century at Bath against Lancashire in 1909, a match which the visitors won by 9 runs and in which J.C.White made his debut for Somerset. It was Daniell's considerable influence within Somerset cricket that was instrumental in maintaining the tradition of fielding numerous amateurs in the side right up to the end of the 1930s.

In the days when sporting seasons were more clearly defined than at present, it was possible for a gifted sportsman who was a cricketer in the summer to pursue his talents at another sport when the cricket season had ended. Thus it is not surprising to learn that many of the Bath personalities who played for Somerset up to the 1950s were also playing rugby for Bath at the other end of the Rec in the winter. John Daniell captained Bath and England at rugby, and later in his life became President of the Rugby Football Union. Other Somerset cricketers who played rugby for Bath included Ulick Considine, a three-quarter who also played for England, Bertie Buse, Jack MacBryan and Louis Powell. There were also R.A.Gerrard, an England rugby international, and Dennis Silk; both played cricket for Somerset but not at Bath. Sammy Woods, too, played rugby for Cambridge University, Somerset and England but not for Bath.

Another who gave a lifetime of service to Somerset cricket was Bath solicitor E.F. 'Bunty' Longrigg. His playing career stretched from 1925 to 1947 and included over 200 matches, and he captained the side from 1938 to 1946 (although there was no county cricket during wartime, when Longrigg was serving as a major). Passing his Law Society Finals in June 1931, he was reported in the Bath Chronicle as receiving 'the congratulations on his success from many friends including members of the Somerset Cricket team for whom he was playing on the Rec this week'. His achievement in the law exams was not matched by his batting in the game against Middlesex, Longrigg making only 6 and 4, but thanks to some fine bowling by Andrews, Wellard and J.C.White, Somerset eventually won by over 100 runs. Longrigg did, however, make many useful runs for Somerset at Bath; he scored a century against Kent in 1930, his innings against Surrey in 1933 is noted elsewhere (in Chapter 12), and his 56 runs contributed to the defeat of Leicestershire in the last Bath Festival match before the Second World War.

Longrigg's services to Somerset cricket continued long after his retirement as a player. He was Chairman of the County for the whole of the 1960s and later became President, an office which his father had held before him. The 1960s were a period of considerable financial anxiety for Somerset with annual losses at the end of the decade running at over £10,000. Various expedients were tried, including the reduction of membership subscriptions to £1 in 1967, in an attempt to encourage the public to join and support the club in large numbers. Somerset also benefited from a windfall legacy of over £10,000 arising from the sale of a stamp collection owned by the pathologist at Bath's Royal United Hospital and this provided a temporary respite. A fundamental improvement in the position only occurred with Max Jeffrey's initiatives in attracting commercial sponsorship for the County and this coincided with a period of greater success on the field in the 1970s.

Max, who was chairman of a Businessmens' Club in Bath started encouraging local companies to support the Bath Cricket Festival by persuading twenty businessmen to donate £10 each for the use of a marquee and enclosure for one day of the Festival. From this small beginning, corporate hospitality had risen to over £35,000 by the end of the 1980s. Having presided also over the successful staging at Bath of two matches against the Australians, including the famous victory of 1977, it was fitting that Max Jeffrey should be Chairman of Somerset during 1979-82, the most successful seasons in the Club's history when four limited overs competitions were won.

Success in those competitions was in some measure attributable to the brilliant batting of Vivian Richards, later captain of the West Indian side, and in 2000 designated as one of Wisden's Five Cricketers of the Century. It was another man of Bath Len Creed, for many years President of the Somerset County Cricket Supporters' Club and later Chairman of the County in 1977 and 1978, who on a holiday in Antigua had seen Richards play and had the inspiration (and personal finance) to persuade the young West Indian to come over to Somerset and take his chance in county cricket, providing him initially with cricket and work at the Lansdown club, until the Somerset Committee could be persuaded to recruit him as their overseas player for 1974. One of the finest of batsmen in all forms of cricket, Richards had thirteen seasons at Somerset playing over 200 county championship matches in which he scored 47 centuries and averaged 50 runs an innings.

Although all Somerset supporters remember Vivian Richards' innings of 322 scored in just under five hours against Warwickshire at Taunton in 1985, spectators at Bath recall with particular pleasure his many match-winning innings in limited overs games and, in the County Championship, his centuries at Bath against Yorkshire (1974), Nottinghamshire (1981) and Kent (1986), all of which contributed to Somerset wins, as well as his major part in the victories there over Glamorgan (1974), the Australians (1977) and Lancashire (1978 and 1985).

Another West Indian with a strong Bath connection is Peter Wight who, after a career with Somerset during which he scored nearly 17,000 runs (with four of his 27 centuries for the County being scored on the Rec), established an indoor cricket coaching school in the city; and one who attended at that school, while living in Bath, was Peter Roebuck, captain of Somerset from 1986-88. Roebuck ended his 18 -year career with the County in 1991 with the fourth highest career aggregate of runs, but of his 31 centuries for Somerset, only one was made at Bath.

The mantle of Len Creed and Max Jeffrey has to a large extent devolved upon Robert and Sylvia Appleyard

Len Creed with Viv Richards

who in recent years have taken prime responsibility for running the Festival. In addition to their duties during the Festival, Sylvia's contribution to the cause of Somerset Cricket has included acting as Secretary to the Bath Area Committee for most of the last 20 years; and all supporters of the Bath Cricket Festival were delighted to hear that Robert's hard work for the County had been recognised with his appointment as Vice-Chairman of Somerset County Cricket Club in 1999.

CHAPTER 12

CATCHES WIN MATCHES

WHEN FANNY BURNEY ATTENDED A CONCERT at a private house in Bath in 1780, she made a diary note of the event in the following terms: '...the young ladies sang catches; oh such singing! worse squalling, more out of tune never did I hear'. In cricket, of course, a catch is not a song sung in succession, but a word applied to one of the methods by which a batsman may be dismissed. The concerted screech of 'Owzatt', by wicket-keeper and cordon of slip fielders when appealing to the umpire for a snick catch behind the wicket is not, however, so far removed from Miss Burney's description of the catches she heard in Bath. There is an old cricket proverb which says that 'Catches win Matches' and this Chapter highlights a selection of incidents relating to catches at the Rec.

One of Somerset's most memorable victories at Bath occurred in June 1901 when Lancashire were defeated by an innings, a match more fully described in Chapter 4. Although the Somerset score eventually totalled over 500, the foundation of the success was laid by a first wicket partnership of over 200 between Lionel Palairet and Len Braund. Palairet was dropped in the slips when his score was 20, and he went on to score 182. This costly miss by Lancashire was compounded by the excellence of the Somerset fielding, when Lancashire were batting, three catches being held by Braund and by the wicket-keeper, the Reverend A.P.Wickham, and two by Sammy Woods.

In the twenty-one seasons between the First and Second World Wars, Surrey came to Bath on four occasions. Somerset's win in 1920 (covered in Chapter 10) was the highlight of their season, 'as gratifying as it was unexpected', in the words of Wisden. Len Braund, always reckoned as one of the County's finest fielders, with 355 catches throughout his Somerset career, did not however take a catch in this game. One who did was Mr Philip Foy, a brilliant catch of his accounting for Andrew Sandham. The captain of Bath Cricket Club Stanley Amor, who was keeping wicket for Somerset, dismissed Herbert Strudwick with a catch and then stumped Jack Hobbs off the bowling of J.C.White. Throughout the match, White bowled 57 overs and finished with 4 wickets for 88, testimony to his remarkable accuracy and control. As the tension mounted during Surrey's second innings, catches were dropped (two by Mr Foy), but he caught one and two others were held, and ultimately victory was secured.

Two years later Surrey exacted revenge with a comprehensive win by 221 runs. Jack Hobbs, having been dismissed for 30 and having retired to a quiet end of the Rec to smoke a contemplative pipe, devoted his time instead, with his customary courtesy, to signing autographs for an army of small boys who besieged him. The match was effectively won for Surrey by Hitch, who hit 107 runs in 70 minutes. In Surrey's second innings, their captain Percy Fender was dismissed when he was caught on the boundary by one of his own colleagues, who was fielding as substitute for an injured Somerset man.

This unusual occurrence was repeated eleven years later when Surrey visited Bath in July 1933. In the first innings, the Surrey opening batsman R.J.Gregory was dismissed when he was caught by one of his own team who was assisting Somerset by fielding as substitute for their injured captain Ingle. Percy Fender was still playing for Surrey at that time, and greatly enlivened proceedings by hitting 66 out of 83 in just under one hour, but their captain that season was Douglas Jardine, who in the previous winter had been involved in the controversy over 'bodyline bowling' when he led England to victory in Australia.

In the same match at Bath in July 1933, Jardine featured in a curious incident. Having scored a couple of fours off the bowling of Tom Young, Jardine played a hard low return to the bowler who immediately threw the ball in the air and appealed for the catch. The umpire at the bowler's end, Patsy Hendren, had his view obscured by Young himself, so the other umpire was asked to adjudicate. He, too, was unable to decide as a fielder had moved in front of him at the crucial moment; so Jardine, having appeared at first to withdraw, remained at the wicket. Shortly afterwards, Young had him caught at the wicket by Wally Luckes for 26. This match, which was rain-affected, was a personal triumph for Bath and Somerset batsman E.F.Longrigg, who with crisp drives and superb placing scored 124 runs; in addition, his catch to remove the Surrey batsman Squires was described, in the words of the Bath Chronicle, as 'a brilliant effort; he ran right round the wicket to achieve it with one hand stretched right out'.

In a national context, the most memorable of all these Somerset v Surrey encounters at Bath was that played in May 1923, for it was in that match that Jack

Hobbs scored his hundredth hundred and helped Surrey to an exciting win by 10 runs. Hobbs' famous innings (116 not out) is covered in Chapter 6, but in the first innings he was brilliantly caught in the gully by John Daniell for nought.

From Somerset's viewpoint, the victory over Gloucestershire in July 1935 will have given particular satisfaction. Needing 101 runs to win in the fourth innings of a match dominated by the bowling of Andrews and Wellard (with an useful 4 for 10 from Harold Gimblett's medium pace in the second innings) Somerset struggled to 85 for 9. It was then that Horace Hazell, who had shared in a last-wicket stand of over 50 with Wally Luckes in the first innings, came to the wicket to join Mr.C.C.C.Case. The latter was unwell and was using Bertie Buse as his runner. Before Hazell had scored, 'Box' Case gave a catch to Stephens at backward short leg. Stephens has already caught Longrigg and Luckes in this second innings, but this time the fielder appeared to snatch at it and the ball fell to the ground. Case thereafter defended stoutly (he was once described by Robertson-Glasgow as a 'miracle of vigilance'), but it was Hazell who scored the runs, finishing with 13 not out. Somerset thus won by one wicket, and in the words of the Bath Chronicle 'it was a refreshing experience to see the spectators rush on the field to cheer Hazell and Case as they went to the pavilion and to give Somerset an approving shout for their performance'.

When Gloucestershire next appeared in Bath at Whitsun 1958, the crowd on the Bank Holiday Monday was one of the largest ever seen at the Rec, an estimated nine thousand people being in the ground. When Somerset began their first innings reply to their visitors' score of 133, the first wicket fell when opening batsman Peter Wight was caught by Arthur Milton, fielding at backward short-leg, off the bowling of Smith for 9. The catch was close to the ground and involved Milton in a turn and dive, ultimately grasping the ball inches from the ground. More than one commentator described the catch as 'brilliant', and this was the first of four catches taken by Milton in this innings. Wight himself held nearly 200 catches for Somerset during his career, one of the most memorable being the running catch, taken at full stretch, which dismissed Alan Jones off Alley's bowling in the County's victory over Glamorgan at the Rec in 1962.

Of the 20 Somerset wickets to fall in a day in the match against Lancashire in 1953, fourteen batsmen were dismissed by catches, eleven of them off the bowling of Tattersall. Brian Langford, who made his first appearance for Somerset in that match, took his first wicket in county cricket on that occasion, having Brian Statham caught by Maurice Tremlett. In the following two matches of the Bath Festival, the

S.M.J. Woods and Rev. A.P. Wickham return to the field after the tea interval; Somerset v Lancashire, June 1901.

young off- spinner took 14 for 156 off 80 overs against Kent, and 11 for 134 off 51 overs against Leicestershire. Of those 26 wickets taken by Brian Langford in the June 1953 Bath Festival, 20 resulted from catches, nine of which were made by Harold Gimblett, fielding at short leg or in the slips.

Most catches are taken by wicket-keepers, and those which Harold Stephenson made, standing up to the wicket off the bowling of Brian Langford, to dismiss first Close and then Taylor of Yorkshire contributed greatly to Somerset's victory on that memorable day in August 1959. 'Superb' was the adjective used in one national newspaper report to describe Stephenson's performance behind the stumps on that day.

A special memory for Bath spectator Jack Blanchard was of the catch taken by Joel Garner in his first match for Somerset, against the Australians in May 1977. The Australian captain Greg Chappell, who had scored a century in his first innings, had made 36 in the second when he was tempted to hook a short ball from Ian Botham; Joel Garner was fielding on the boundary at long leg just in front of the spectators and Jack remembers Garner appearing merely to stretch out his hand to gather the catch.

When Middlesex appeared at Bath in June 1987, a gem of a personal contest took place between England off-spinner John Emburey and Somerset's New Zealand Test Match batsman, Martin Crowe. In the first innings, Crowe had hit Emburey for three successive fours and looked to be winning this particular duel. But as The Times cricket correspondent John Woodcock reported: 'it was Emburey who had the last word, Crowe being caught at the wicket, pushing out at the arm ball. It was the classic off- spinner's dismissal'. Emburey finished with 5 for 60 in 35 overs, but Crowe won the battle in the second innings, scoring 102 not out in another rain-affected match which ended in a draw.

Six years later, Middlesex again visited Bath for the first four-day game to be played there. The 1993 County Championship was the first to consist entirely of four-day games, introduced to give a batsman the opportunity to build a longer innings and to make bowlers contrive to be more resourceful in bowling teams out. In an effort to secure a result, after time had been lost due to rain, Middlesex declared their first innings closed and the two captains Chris Tavaré and John Carr agreed that Middlesex would be set a target in a certain minimum number of overs. Somerset scored freely in their second innings, the front-line Middlesex bowlers being replaced by Carr and Haynes whose 18 overs yielded 134 runs. When Somerset's last batsman (and renowned big-hitter) André van Troost came to the wicket, he hit a slow long hop from Carr straight to Haynes on the boundary. In the words of Wisden: 'Carr shouted 'drop it', because he had already agreed with Somerset captain Tavaré, what the victory target would be. Haynes, however, caught it. And, though there was no audible appeal, umpire Meyer ruled that van Troost was out'. The celebrated West Indian opening batsman Desmond Haynes, having taken the catch, then went on to win the match for Middlesex with a second innings score of 115, and Middlesex in due course ended the 1993 season as County Champions.

CHAPTER 13

The Recreation Ground

THE REC IS A GROUND OF CONSIDERABLE NATURAL BEAUTY, its position enhanced by its proximity to the centre of the city. Surrounded by hills in the background, by the Georgian splendour of Great Pulteney Street on one side and by the River Avon on another, it is only the Sports Hall at the North Parade end, a faceless, unattractive building, which detracts somewhat from the overall beauty of the setting; and even the view towards the Sports Hall has been improved by the construction of an elegant new stand at one end of the Rugby ground, with tented roofs in moorish style.

The entrance to the Rec from the Great Pulteney Street end is guarded by a gateway having two wrought-iron turnstiles, each backed by a small wooden pavilion sufficient to house a gate-keeper. They serve no purpose now but remain as a reminder of past days. The ground has a small cricket pavilion, with a terracotta tiled roof and bell- tower, for use as a changing area by players during the course of a match. Both the cricket pavilion and gateway date back to the 1890s when the Rec was first created as a sports ground.

The Bath and County Recreation Ground Company Limited originally took a 21 year lease of the whole area from Captain Forester, the owner of much of the Bathwick Estate. After the First World War, the Company acquired the land from him and retained title to the Rec until it was sold to the Bath City Council in 1956. The area on which the Recreation Ground stands is a fairly flat plain, consisting of mixed sands, clays and gravel, over a bedrock of Lias clay. Various drainage systems were built by the Georgians and Victorians across this plain, but it was not until the flood control work carried out in the 1970s that the problem of flooding receded. Even then, heavy rain in June 1980 caused the abandonment of the scheduled match against Lancashire.

*Bert Lock
inspects the
Bath wicket.*

The preparation of a good cricket pitch involves a combination of science, art and a measure of luck. At the beginning, the Recreation Ground Company employed the services of George Hearne to make the ground and pitches suitable for first-class cricket. More recently, and at least over the last fifty years, the pitches at Bath have been prepared under the supervision of the Somerset County Groundsmen, from Cecil Buttle to Phil Frost. Over the years, the Bath pitches have received their share of criticism, sometimes being described euphemistically as 'sporting', but they have as often been praised, and recent reports have declared them to be excellent. Traditionally, Bath pitches were always regarded as low and slow, with the ball coming on to the bat slower, leaving a bowler with less margin for error.

Lancashire captain Cyril Washbrook certainly expressed doubts as to the suitability of the wicket in 1953, when the pitch had been re-laid after the previous summer, and his doubts proved well-founded, the match finishing inside a day with Lancashire the winners by an innings. The following match of the 1953 Festival also threatened to be completed early. Derek Ufton, who was playing for Kent, recalled how on the first day, a Wednesday, Somerset had been dismissed for 123 and Kent, in reply, had reached 153 for 8 by the close. The position was even worse for Somerset than such statistics would suggest for Maurice Tremlett, their captain, had been badly injured by a blow on the head when fielding and would take no further part in the game, and newcomer Clive Davey had also been injured in the field. After Somerset's batting disaster five days earlier against Lancashire, the Kent players did not expect the game to last through the course of the Thursday, and accordingly checked out of the Royal York Hotel on the morning of the second day.

Strange things happen in cricket and Somerset's fortunes were transformed on that second day. After getting Kent all out for 178, giving the visitors a lead of 55, Somerset proceeded to make a mockery of all their batting difficulties of the past few

The flooded Rec during Bath Cricket Week, June 1903.

innings. With centuries from Gimblett and Buse, and a score of 65 from Johnny Lawrence, Somerset batted through the day. The Kent players returned to the Royal York Hotel to find that the rooms which they had relinquished that morning had all been taken; the hotel did manage to find two or three rooms for them which meant that the players slept four or five to a room! On the third day, Somerset completed their victory by 153 runs, Brian Langford taking 6 for 60 in the second innings to add to his 8 for 96 in the first.

According to local tradition, the reason for the pitch lasting longer through the Kent match after the disaster of the game against Lancashire was that Johnny Lawrence had the inspired idea of suggesting that a mixture of marl and water be prepared to create a paste to be rolled into the wicket to bind the surface.

The Recreation Ground is low-lying and stands close to the River Avon. On four occasions during the long history of the Bath Cricket Festival, a match has had to be abandoned without a ball being bowled. The most dramatic of these cancellations occurred in 1968 when, for the second part of the Festival in July, over three thousand deck chairs were transported from Taunton to provide seating for spectators at the Rec. When the River Avon burst its banks and flooded the ground, the deck chairs floated away down the river. The Committee were also concerned about the portable covers for the wickets, which were the only ones possessed, and which were in danger also of floating away. Max Jeffrey remembered that his car was the last one remaining on the ground, and when he went to collect it, it was standing in water up to its hub caps.

Immediately before this flood, a pitch inspector had been called after the match against Hampshire in 1968, when both captains had complained to the umpires about the state of the wicket but any immediate problem was resolved by the flood. By the following year, appropriate surgery had brought the pitches again up to the required standard.

Numerous are the occasions when rain has delayed or curtailed play at the Rec. Such interruptions are a hazard of all cricket matches and are not unique to Bath. Indeed in 1933, Bath was being congratulated on achieving two and a half hours play on a day when at four other venues, rain prevented any play at all. When Surrey visited Bath in that year, their captain Douglas Jardine was reported to be astonished to find play delayed by rain. 'I thought Bath weather was so wonderful, I often see its sunshine figures', he said.

In addition to the problems of the weather, all festival cricket involves the hazards of temporary structures. Before the building of the Sports Hall and the large

David Oldam, Somerset scorer from 1983 to 1998, at work at the Rec.

Rugby Stand parallel to the river, it was possible for spectators on North Parade Bridge to obtain a free, if somewhat distant, view of the cricket. At various times, more than one hundred people have been counted indulging in this pastime, and to restrict this luxury, a large screen was from time to time erected in the south-west corner of the Rec. Such a structure often caused more trouble than it was worth, as in 1923 when the screen collapsed in a gale. There was more drama in 1988 when strong winds threatened to blow down one of the sight-screens. Four of the poles holding the screen bent at right-angles and workmen had to be called in at night to repair the structure in time for the resumption of play in the morning.

In the past, the Press and Scorers had a tent which was usually located to the west of the Pavilion, and was thus often vulnerable to big hits which landed with a thud on to the roof of the tent. Accommodation for the journalists and scorers is now provided in a portable cabin on top of the temporary administration offices. Although the old-fashioned score book is still used, it is supplemented by sophisticated electronic equipment.

In the 1990s, the re-siting of the square further away from where Bath Rugby play had a beneficial effect on the quality of the pitches, and also resulted in an improvement in the condition of the outfield. Since the introduction of the four-day game, the pitch has been ideal for championship cricket and at the Festival in 2000 it was rated excellent and given the highest grade by the officials.

CHAPTER 14

SETTING UP THE FESTIVAL

THE RECREATION GROUND, as its name suggests, is an area for recreation. At various times through the year, cricket, croquet, hockey, lawn tennis and rugby are, or have been, played there. The Rec is not a purpose-built cricket ground, with stands for spectators, administration buildings, and indoor training areas and treatment rooms for the players. For every Bath Cricket Festival, the Rec has to be prepared, not only on the ground and pitch for the cricket, but also with facilities for players and spectators, although in recent years Bath Rugby Club have generously offered their clubhouse for the provision of lunches and teas.

The preparation for the annual Cricket Festival starts with the allocation by Somerset County Cricket Club (usually in the autumn of the previous year) of the matches to be played in Bath. The local Bath Area Committee meets throughout the year to plan for the Festival and in January, the tenders go out and orders are placed with the suppliers of the services and equipment required for the coming summer, such as seating, stewarding and supplies.

One of the first decisions to be taken concerns the provision of tiered seating and marquee tents. For the Festival of 1898, a temporary grandstand was erected, and for the matches against Australia in 1972 and 1977 similar arrangements were made. Hospitality tents and marquees have frequently adorned the ground, and recently tiered seating has regularly been provided for members and the general public.

The securing of, and arrangements for, corporate hospitality has for the past few years been dealt with by the full-time marketing manager at Taunton, Gianna Tesser. While this has lifted a major responsibility from the shoulders of the local Area Committee, its members still maintain an important role in meeting representatives of the Bath Chamber of Commerce and in canvassing support for the Festival from local businesses. During the Festival too, much remains to be done on the spot at the Rec, and Area Committee member Chris May has in recent years had a particular responsibility for this.

Although the parks department of Bath and North East Somerset Council maintains the Rec throughout the year, the Somerset head groundsman Phil Frost visits periodically to monitor the condition of the ground. Over recent years the pattern has been that some two weeks before the beginning of the Festival, Phil Frost and his team arrive from Taunton to finalise the prepararation of the pitches. They are followed, about a week before the scheduled start, by Robin Arnold and his team who for the past ten years have set up and connected the basic supplies required of water and electricity, and who begin the task of converting the Rec into an arena suitable for first-class cricket; a little later the temporary structures for offices for administration arrive. This is followed by the erection of the marquees and ancillary facilities for the corporate hospitality areas; at the same time, the stands, seats, portable lavatories, sightscreens (now also requiring black covering for the limited overs games), refreshment tents, and umpires' caravan arrive for installation, together with the barriers to segregate areas and equipment. Pallets, too, have often to be sited to raise the height of seats; and all suppliers have to be instructed where to locate their goods and equipment. For the duration of the Festival and for the week before it starts, an increasing security presence is required to supervise the ground. Shortly before the start of the Festival, car parking areas have to be marked out and the stewards briefed as to their particular duties; these aspects of the Festival organisation have lately been undertaken by Area Committee members Rowland Bartlett and Graham Ward. With room for the parking of several hundred cars on the Rec, problems encountered by Rowland's team are somewhat different from those faced by stewards 50 years ago. Then it was necessary to insist that

Charlie Bishop.

Sylvia Sims picks the lucky winner of the Grand Draw, with Ann Meddings (Theatre Royal), Sylvia Appleyard, Robert Appleyard and Peter Yeman.

cars were parked back to the pitch. If a car were parked front on, looking straight at the wicket, it was regarded as a 'grandstand' for entertainment tax purposes, and the County Club was liable to a tax of two-pence a car.

Although personnel have from time to time been recruited locally, the stewards from the County Ground at Taunton normally come to Bath to help with the Cricket Festival; among these can be counted legendary characters like Charlie Bishop, nicknamed 'the oldest bouncer in the west'. In 1992, at the age of 84, Charlie was celebrating his sixteenth consecutive year as a steward at the Bath Festival.

Before spectators can be admitted to the Festival, the requirements of the Health and Safety Executive have to be observed, which involve inspection by an official of the HSE, and the issue of a compliance certificate. A responsible official of the Club has to be designated as 'Health and Safety Officer', a role fulfilled recently by Sylvia Appleyard. No longer can children sit on the grass behind a rope to watch the cricket. The boundary is now designated by perimeter advertising boards, all of which are transported by lorry, together with much other equipment, from the Taunton ground. But the boundary boards do perform an additional function. They act as a long-stop to the numerous informal games, with bat and ball, in which the successors to Tennyson's 'herd of boys, who with clamour bowled and stumped the wicket' participate during the lunch and tea intervals on the grass at all Festival matches.

To ensure that everything runs smoothly for the Festival, the members of the local Area Committee undertake numerous duties each day, from dealing with enquiries and the liaising with the Council and the Rugby Club, to the monitoring of supplies and the drying and putting out of chairs for spectators; important guests and potential sponsors also need to be entertained. To assist with the organisation, a large number of staff come from County headquarters in Taunton. At the conclusion of the Festival, everything is dismantled, equipment is returned to suppliers or to Taunton, and life on the Rec returns to normal.

The first Bath Cricket Festival was a joint venture between the Bath and

Bath Area Committee members with Cllr. David Hawkins at Bath Guildhall, 1997.

County Recreation Ground Company Limited and the Somerset County Cricket Club, where the Company provided the Ground and facilities and Somerset organised the cricket; the income from spectators was shared between the Company and the Club. More recently, the Festival has been organised by the County through its Bath Area Committee, with a significant involvement of the local Council. The interest of the local Council in the Festival has been further strenghtened by the presence on the Area Committee of Councillor David Hawkins, who has been a member of the Bath and North East Somerset Council for many years and was its Chairman in 1997.

In 1920, the receipts for the Cricket Festival week (two matches) were put at £450, thought to be somewhat lower than expected, possibly on account of two of the days clashing with the Bath Races. In 1950, receipts from three games were just under £2,000. By 1984, income from the two county matches and two limited overs games which comprised the Bath Cricket Festival was around £21,500 and the cost of staging the Festival was estimated at £20,000. At that time the local Council charged Somerset County Cricket Club a rent for the hire of the Ground. In 2000, the cost of staging the Festival was estimated at £50,000. Income is now derived mainly from the hire of marquees for corporate hospitality and the sale of catering franchises. This is supplemented by local fund-raising of £15,000 (including matching finance from Bath and North East Somerset Council), and gate-money from the paying spectators, which has averaged £13,500 for the last two years.

The days when some 9,000 spectators attended to see Somerset play Gloucestershire on Whit-Monday 1958 (and some 4,000 official scorecards were sold) are over; crowds of that size no longer attend Bath or any other ground for county cricket. Apart from many more rival attractions, safety requirements are far more stringent and higher standards of comfort are demanded now than were necessary or indeed could be found in the post-war years. Hence the stands of tiered seating in place of the benches (or grass) which sufficed fifty years ago. To attract a crowd of 5,000 spectators to the Rec for a day's cricket now would be regarded as a major achievement.

Writing in 1990 the Somerset Chief Executive Peter Anderson paid tribute to the sterling efforts of the local Area Committee in organising the Cricket Festival in these terms: 'A lot of unpaid work goes into staging the event, the bulk of which is carried out by the Bath Area Committee Members. Duties range from menial tasks such as loading/unloading chairs and supplies to security and cleaning duties..... Max Jeffrey, a former chairman of the County Club, has continued in his role of raising sponsorship which basically underwrites the cost of staging the Festival......Bob Doel for the second year running is co-ordinating the Festival on the Recreation Ground.....It means he has to spend a week there before the Festival starts and then supervise the packing up after it ends. As you can see then, the County Club is indebted to the Bath Area Committee for staging the Festival'.

Although the individuals have changed, Peter Anderson's words were as true in 2000 as they were in 1990. The bare outline given earlier in this Chapter of the work involved in setting up the Festival reveals the range of tasks and duties to which people like Bob Doel, Peter Yeman, David Watts, Robert and Sylvia Appleyard, all from the local Area Committee and all acting as volunteers have, in the past decade, devoted weeks of their respective lives. Fifteen years ago, it was John Young who was primarily responsible for organising the Festival.

Fifty years ago Major Wade, Honorary Secretary of the Bath Area for nearly 25 years, was in charge, and in the 1920s Mr F.E. Rogers and Mr. R.F.A.Farnham supervised the setting up of the Festival. Bath has been fortunate to have so many willing volunteers to devote their enthusiasm and to commit their time to continue the Festival tradition.

CHAPTER 15

THE LAST HALF CENTURY

AFTER SOME SUCCESS IN 1946, the first season after the war, when three wins at Bath were achieved and the County finished fourth, the results of the next ten seasons were mixed. For the first five years, although the County ended the season mostly in the lower half of the table, an average of seven wins a season was attained. These were years when some of the pre-war stalwarts, Bertie Buse, Harold Gimblett, Horace Hazell and Arthur Wellard were still playing, as was R.J.O.Meyer, an amateur all-rounder, who captained Somerset in 1947. The nadir was reached in the 'Surrey Years' of 1952-55. In each of these four years, Surrey won the Championship and Somerset finished last, winning only two Championship matches each season. Surrey continued their winning ways, taking the title in the following three seasons to achieve a record seven in a row, and by 1958, the fortunes of Somerset, under the captaincy of Maurice Tremlett, were on the rise. In that year Somerset, with twelve victories, achieved third place in the table.

Tremlett had started playing for the County just after the war, primarily as a fast- medium bowler. He suffered a fearful injury when he was struck in the face, fielding at silly mid-off, in the match against Kent at the Rec in June 1953. He played no more that year, but returned to the side as a batsman, and in 1956 was appointed captain of the County, the first professional to be so honoured. By 1958, with the arrival of the two Australians, Bill Alley and Colin McCool, and supported by Peter Wight, Geoff Lomax, Brian Langford and the ever reliable Harold Stephenson behind the wicket, Tremlett had not only a talented, but a more settled team, most of these men playing in every match.

Up to 1957, Somerset were playing three first-class matches in Bath, usually over a consecutive ten day period, and always in June, though occasionally ending

Harold Stephenson leads Somerset into the field against Gloucestershire, 4 June 1960.

at the beginning of July. In 1958 and for the next three years, four championship matches were played at the Rec and these were split between two weeks, the first occurring in May or June and the second in July or August. These were years when the number of Championship matches was increased from 28 to 32 a season, so with at least 16 games, Somerset home matches were played at a host of venues around the County. In 1960, Somerset staged their home matches at Taunton (6), Bath (4), Weston-super-Mare (3), and one each at Bristol (Imperial), Glastonbury and Yeovil.

In the twenty seasons from 1946 to 1965, Somerset won 27 and lost 25 of their County Championship matches played at the Rec, with 9 matches ending in a draw. In addition, there were in the late 1940s, four matches against Cambridge and Oxford Universities, resulting in one win and two losses for Somerset, with one draw.

By 1960, Harold Stephenson had taken over the captaincy, to be succeeded later by Colin Atkinson. At Bath in 1962, when Nottinghamshire were defeated, Stephenson made the highest score of his career (147 not out), and against Glamorgan in the same year he achieved six dismissals in an innings, five being catches off the bowling of Ken Palmer. Colin Atkinson's finest performance at Bath was an innings of 89 against Gloucestershire in 1966, a match eventually won for Somerset by the combined spin bowling of Peter Robinson (8 for 99) and Brian Langford (10 for 82).

In July 1966, the England Football team won the World Cup. A less memorable happening occurred that year, one which demonstrated the pressure faced by the Cricket authorities to maintain and increase the popularity of the game as the Nation's major summer sport. The Committee charged with examining the future of county cricket, and particularly with making it more appealing to the spectator, recommended that, as an experiment, the first innings should be limited to 65 overs for some of the county matches (12 for each county). The recommendation was expected to produce more entertaining cricket and give first day spectators an opportunity to see both teams bat. Other benefits forecast for the experiment were that it would encourage more spin bowling and lead to the production of improved pitches.

Curiously, of Somerset's three matches at Bath during that season, those where the first innings was limited to 65 overs, against Gloucestershire and Surrey, were both won by Somerset, whereas the game against Kent, played under 'normal' playing conditions, was lost. It was a wet summer in 1966, and the experiment was discontinued at the end of the season. By the end of the decade, the image of cricket was being re-packaged with the introduction of another limited overs game.

The 1960s had started at the Rec with a third wicket stand of 300 between Graham Atkinson (190) and Peter Wight (155 not out) against Glamorgan, a record Somerset partnership for any wicket which was to stand for 20 years. These two, with Bill Alley, Mervyn Kitchen and Roy Virgin, formed the backbone of the Somerset batting at this time and all had memorable innings at Bath. The bowling was in the capable hands of Fred Rumsey and Brian Langford, and of those two formidable all-rounders, Bill Alley and Ken Palmer. Brian Langford made his debut for Somerset at the age of seventeen in the Bertie Buse benefit match against Lancashire in 1953, and he recalled that he was selected for that match only because Johnny Lawrence had to be released to go home to Yorkshire on account of the death of his father. Langford ended his career in 1974 having played in more matches for Somerset (504) than anyone else. During 18 seasons of Somerset cricket at Bath, from 1953 and then, after a two year interval for National Service, from 1956 to 1972, Brian Langford bowled in 55 matches at Bath and collected 217 wickets at an average of 17 runs per wicket.

The year of the great flood, 1968, was one when four matches were scheduled for Bath. The first two in June ended in a draw with Essex and a loss against Hampshire, for whom Bob Cottam, who later coached at Somerset, had match fig-

Bill Alley
bowling at Bath.

ures of 8 for 81. For the proposed July Festival, the match scheduled against Derbyshire was abandoned without a ball being bowled and with the Bath ground flooded, the following match, against Warwickshire, was transferred to Taunton. Cottam
returned the following year with Hampshire and took 5 for 48 off 31 overs as
Somerset struggled to 197 in their second innings to set the visitors a target of 170 to
win. Hampshire failed by two runs, the Somerset hero on this occasion being Ken
Palmer, who had match figures of 7 for 92 off 40 overs, to add to his 37 not out in the
second innings.

Among the great England cricketers of the post-war era who came to Bath
as visitors, it was the bowlers who were more prominent and successful than the
batsmen. Brian Statham had match figures of 6 for 37 in 1950, 4 for 27 in 1953 and 8
for 66 in 1954 to help Lancashire to three victories at the Rec, while Trevor Bailey,
with 5 for 17 and 2 for 51, plus an innings of 18, was instrumental in securing an
innings win for Essex in 1951, a match in which Bath-born Jim Redman took three
wickets in nine balls. Fred Trueman, with match figures of 6 for 45 off 31 overs, put
Yorkshire on the road to victory in 1958, despite a last wicket stand of 84 between

Geoff Lomax (94 not out) and Brian Lobb (42), the highest ever tenth wicket stand for Somerset at Bath; and although Frank Tyson captured only two wickets off 20 overs in 1960, it was Northamptonshire who won the contest.

Of the slow bowlers who visited Bath, D.V.P.Wright, the Kent and England wrist- spinner, had match figures of 10 for 100 in 1951 (to add to his figures of 16 for 80 in 1939), but on neither occasion were Kent able to force a win. Derek Underwood, with 11 for 133 in 1966 was more successful in bowling Kent to their first win at Bath for over 30 years. In 1959, the great Surrey spin bowling pair of Laker and Lock bowled more than 100 overs in the match to secure a Surrey win by 10 wickets, Laker's match figures being 9 for 122. (On that occasion, Surrey's acting captain Alec Bedser took 4 for 73 in the Somerset first innings, opening the bowling with Peter Loader).

The other outstanding off-spinner to enjoy coming to Bath in those days was Fred Titmus who had made his debut at the Rec (aged 16) for Middlesex in 1949, and whose match figures of 10 for 84 in Middlesex's win in 1954 were eclipsed the following year when he took 15 for 95. In 1955, however, the victory went to Somerset.

Spectators at Bath were less lucky with a sight of the leading English batsmen of the post-war years. Len Hutton scored only 3 on his one appearance at the Rec (in 1936), and Yorkshire did not re-appear there until 1958, by which time Hutton had retired. His opening partner for England Cyril Washbrook, made 91 in 1950 and 118 in 1954, and John Edrich scored an 80 and a 60 in four matches for Surrey. Dennis Amiss, Denis Compton, Colin Cowdrey, Ted Dexter and Peter May never played at the Rec. But one England player who did succeed with both bat and ball was Brian Close, who made a century at Bath in 1959, scored lots of runs in 1964, and took wickets in both games.

After a dispute with Yorkshire, for whom he had played for over 20 years, Brian Close was persuaded by Bill Andrews to continue his career with Somerset. Close was a man used to winning and at 40 years of age believed that he had plenty of cricket left in him. Within a year of his arrival in 1971, he had succeeded Brian Langford as captain and he remained as such for the next six years, which included the two matches against Australia. Close came shortly after Tom Cartwright, who had arrived in 1970 from Warwickshire, and the joint impact of these two on Somerset cricket was immense. Close did not score a century for Somerset at Bath in the County Championship, but he had many fine performances there, and will have derived particular satisfaction from the defeat of Yorkshire in 1974. In the victories at the Rec over Derbyshire (1970), Essex (1971) and Surrey (1973), Tom Cartwright

Vic Marks bowling at the Rec. The umpire is David Shepherd.

made major contributions with bat, ball, or both.

Some of the finest cricketers ever to represent the County emerged during the years of influence of Cartwright and Close at Somerset. This was the time when first Brian Rose, Ian Botham and Vivian Richards, and then a little later in the 1970s, Victor Marks, Peter Roebuck and Joel Garner started playing for Somerset. It was at the end of the 1970s that Somerset achieved success in limited overs matches, reaching the final of the Gillette Cup in 1978, and winning that Cup and the John Player League in 1979. This was followed in 1981 and 1982 by success in the Benson and Hedges Cup Finals, and the following year in the NatWest Trophy, the successor to the Gillette Cup. Together with all the excitement of the limited overs competitions, the position of the County in the Championship was consistently higher. Although Somerset finished at the foot of the table in 1969 and 1985, in the 20 seasons from 1966 to 1985, the County maintained an average of eighth position (half-way) in the Championship table.

At Bath during this period (1966-1985), 45 County Championship matches were staged. Of these, Somerset won 15, lost 6 and drew 22 (with 2 being aban-

Sybil Maunder provides Neil Mallender with a refreshing drink.

doned). One of these draws was enlivened by the fastest century ever scored by a Somerset cricketer. Against Gloucestershire in 1983 Nigel Popplewell scored a century in 41 minutes and when he was finally out for 143, he had been batting for just 62 minutes. In addition, four other first-class matches were played, resulting in two wins for Somerset (against Australia and Cambridge University), one loss (against Pakistan), and one draw with Australia. Many of the outstanding performances by Somerset and other individual players at Bath during this period are covered elsewhere in this book.

By 1985, the number of matches played in the County Championship had fallen to 22- 24, which meant that only two such matches were allocated to Bath each year. The defeat of Kent in 1986 was relished by spectators who saw centuries from Vivian Richards (128) and Brian Rose (107 not out), with fifties from Richard Harden and Victor Marks. These were achieved against a Kent bowling attack which included three England Test Match bowlers, Graham Dilley, Richard Ellison and Derek Underwood, and the Australian International bowler, Terry Alderman. When Kent batted, splendid bowling from Joel Garner (9 for 85), Victor Marks (5 for 108) and a young spinner Richard Coombs (5 for 108) ensured that Kent were dismissed twice.

With the introduction of the four-day game in 1993, the number of county matches played was reduced still further and from that time Bath has staged only one four-day game and one limited overs game during its Festival Week. What the four-day game has usually achieved is a victory for one side, the eight matches played in Bath since 1993 resulting in only one draw. Of the 14 three-day matches played at the Rec between 1986 and 1992, eleven ended as draws.

In the 1990s, Mark Lathwell, Marcus Trescothick and Piran Holloway all achieved at Bath their maiden first-class centuries, and Rob Turner scored centuries in both 1996 and 1999. Mark Lathwell became in 1994 the first Somerset batsman to score 200 at Bath (see Chapter 6), and during this last decade at the Rec, spectators have witnessed outstanding Somerset bowling performances from Neil Mallender, Graham Rose, Mushtaq Ahmed and Andrew Caddick.

At the beginning of the decade, they also had a sight of the batting skills of two of England's major batsmen of this era when Graham Gooch (1990) and David Gower (1991), each of whom played more than one hundred Test Matches for England, came with their respective counties to Bath. Although both had good scores, they were not quite so successful as another England captain Mike Gatting, who earlier had enjoyed himself hugely at Bath. In 1984, he scored 258 runs in one innings, in only 85 overs and including 8 sixes; he followed this three years later, celebrating the announcement of the award to him of an OBE, with an innings of 196. By way of contrast, there could be cited an innings some 20 years earlier of Keith Fletcher, who also captained England in the 1980s, and who batted and battled for six hours at the Rec to score 131 not out to save Essex from defeat in 1968.

CHAPTER 16

LIMITED OVERS CRICKET

LIMITED OVERS CRICKET entered on to the domestic summer programme in 1963, when a knock-out competition was sponsored by Gillette, the sponsorship being taken over some 20 years later by NatWest. The intention was to promote a game which could be completed in one day when each team had allocated to it a maximum number of overs. The participants included all first-class counties, and as the 60 overs competition grew in popularity, it embraced an increasing number of other teams such as Scotland and some of the Minor Counties. Having lost in the Final to Kent in 1967, and to Sussex in 1978, Somerset eventually won the Gillette Cup at Lord's in 1979, defeating Northamptonshire and then went on to win the successor NatWest Trophy in 1983. The only match played at Bath in this cup competition was in 1991 when Somerset won against Buckinghamshire, one of the Minor Counties.

The success of this limited overs format resulted in an agreement between the English Cricket Authorities and the Benson and Hedges tobacco company for the latter to sponsor a new competition starting in 1972 to include all first-class counties and some combined Minor Counties and University teams. This Benson and Hedges cup was won by Somerset two years running, in 1981 and 1982 when first Surrey and then Nottinghamshire were defeated in memorable finals at Lord's. Only one Benson and Hedges match has been played at Bath and that was in May 1977, immediately following Somerset's historic victory against the Australian Touring team. Despite Vivian Richards' scoring 60 not out and winning the Sponsors' Gold Award, Lancashire won the match by 5 wickets.

Between the establishment of these two limited overs competitions, a much shorter match (40 overs per side) was devised especially for play on a Sunday, and another tobacco company, John Player & Sons Limited undertook to sponsor these matches and award prizes. The 'John Player League' – the sponsorship was later taken over by others – became an integral and highly popular part of the Bath Cricket Festival from its inception in 1969, since which date over 40 matches have been staged at the Rec. The first match, in May 1969, was played against Kent who won comfortably, and Somerset ended the

Peter Roebuck.

season in sixteenth position. Over the next five years, as the County gained experience in the competition, five out of the six matches played at Bath were won by Somerset who finished second in 1974. The match at Bath that year was an exciting one in which Yorkshire were defeated by 4 runs with three balls to spare, Brian Close with 131 and Jim Parks with 46 not out being the main scorers. After two defeats in 1975, the next three seasons saw three wins for Somerset, in matches dominated by some big hitting from Ian Botham and Viv Richards.

The first and only time that Somerset won the John Player League was in 1979. In the match at Bath that year, outstanding bowling (by Moseley, Dredge, Burgess, Breakwell and Jennings, none of whom conceded more than 24 runs in their allocated eight overs each) restricted Essex to 120 runs. Somerset succeeded comfortably by 9 wickets, Brian Rose and Peter Denning scoring 109 for the first wicket, and this was one of twelve victories which enabled the County to win the competition. However significant that victory was in the context of the history and achievements of Somerset County Cricket, it is the quartet of matches played in 1982 and 1983, all of which were won by Somerset in spectacular fashion, which will long remain in the memory of spectators at Bath.

Against Surrey in June 1982, Brian Rose and Joel Garner put on 85 runs in 13 overs to win a match which appeared lost when they came together at 94 for 6. Hitting six sixes and two fours, Garner scored his 59 not out off only 48 balls, while

Rose, steadily accumulating runs, finished with 49 not out. The following Sunday, in a rain-affected match against Nottinghamshire restricted to 28 overs per side, Garner clean bowled the last four batsmen to finish with an analysis of four wickets for six runs off six overs.

In a high scoring game in 1983 against Glamorgan, after Nigel Popplewell's innings of 84, it was Peter Roebuck and Colin Dredge, with 30 and 25 respectively (both not out), who secured victory by five wickets with one over to spare. The following Sunday, with Richards and Garner back in the side the day after their West Indies team had lost the World Cup final at Lord's to India, it was a century by Roebuck and an aggressive 73 from Ian Botham followed by some effective bowling by Marks and Popplewell which enabled Somerset to restrict Gloucestershire to 238, and win by 16 runs. Somerset finished second in the John Player League of 1983, as they had done in both 1980 and 1981, when another victory against Gloucestershire had been recorded. This match, in June 1981, was played on the Sunday in the middle of a County Championship match in which Gloucestershire's Pakistani batsman,

Bertie Buse presents Peter Roebuck with a prize, watched by Nigel Popplewell, Peter Denning, Sunil Gavaskar and Brian Rose, June 1980.

Zaheer Abbas, scored 215 and 150, both times not out. In the Sunday match, Zaheer was dismissed (bowled by Botham) for a mere 8 runs.

Roger Sansbury of Bath Cricket Club had a vivid recollection of this match against Gloucestershire in 1981. He was sitting in a radio commentary box doing a broadcast for the benefit of the local Bath hospital. A large crowd had assembled at the Rec on that Sunday for this local derby match. The

Jimmy Cook

commentary box comprised some pieces of scaffolding with a wooden structure at the top and a number of wires. It could not be described as the pinnacle of comfort and had a tendency to sway in the wind but it was a tempting prospect for many whose view of the proceedings on the pitch was limited by the large crowd; thus, Roger's radio commentary was interspersed with commands to budding steeple-jacks to remove themselves at once.

Despite the threatened invasions of his commentary position, Roger remembered the match as a fine game of cricket. Batting first, Somerset ran up a brisk 212 for 7 in their 40 overs, with Peter Roebuck the top scorer with an unbeaten 73. For Gloucestershire, their talented South African all-rounder, Mike Proctor conceded only 28 runs off his 8 overs. In their reply, Gloucestershire steadily took the game over with a fine stand of 118 between Proctor and Andy Stovold. Although Stovold was dismissed for 54, only 30 runs were needed from their last seven wickets with overs in hand. Proctor, however, lost the strike before succumbing, for a brilliant 91, to a smart stumping by Derek Taylor off the bowling of Richards. Roger recalled that there followed a major collapse with batsmen arriving hurriedly at the wicket. Five of these batsmen failed to score, four of them falling to Joel Garner (4 for 20), bowling at his most lethal. Somerset were winners by 20 runs. 'Never in doubt' the locals said!

Whereas through the 1970s only one John Player League match was generally played at Bath, the position throughout the 1980s was that each Bath Festival staged two such games; and of the twenty games played, Somerset won fourteen. Notable achievements included the centuries scored for Somerset in the two victories of 1989 by Chris Tavaré and Jimmy Cook.

Under a new sponsor in 1993, the format of the League was changed from 40 to 50 overs each side, which required a start to the match before lunch. In addition, coloured clothing was introduced in place of the traditional 'whites'. The experiment of 50 overs matches was discontinued for the following season but the other innovations remained. By this time, Bath's allocation of Sunday matches had been reduced to one.

In the last two years, the format of the old John Player League competition has been varied yet again and a new 45 overs game has been introduced, currently called the Norwich Union National Cricket League. While most matches are still played on a Sunday, some are staged mid-week including day/night games played under floodlights. In 1999 and 2000, Somerset won both games staged on Sundays at Bath in this new competition. In the first, against Nottinghamshire, it was Peter Bowler and Piran Holloway who starred with the bat. In the second, against Sussex, it was Marcus Trescothick, hitting four sixes in his innings of 72, and Graham Rose who proved the match-winners on the day. Rose not only bowled economically but his outstanding catch to remove Australian International batsman Michael Bevan effectively ended Sussex hopes of a win.

CHAPTER 17

'FOUR MORE GERANIA, CRUSOE'

SIR NEVILLE CARDUS has long been acknowledged as one of the finest writers on cricket. The October 1967 Edition of Playfair Cricket Monthly published an article by him on 'Gamesmanship' which, he argued, if used with wit, added spice to any sport. To support his argument, Cardus cited in his article the following incident:

'In the 1920s, Yorkshire, playing Somersetshire at Bath, were determined, in the last overs of the game, not to win a first innings decision. At this period in cricket's history, an outright win was worth five points. In drawn games, the side leading on the first innings scored two points. Matches in which no result on the first innings was arrived at had no bearing at all on the Championship. The scoring was reckoned on the percentage of points obtained to points obtainable. Obviously, if rain prevented play at a game's beginning, limiting the issue to a first innings' decision, percentage could suffer if two points were gained out of a 'possible' five. (The system was unfair, because weather frequently did not allow time or scope for the winning of five points.)

So, at Bath, Yorkshire obstinately declined to score and pass Somersetshire's first innings' total. The time of the afternoon reached five minutes to six – five minutes before close of play. Emmott Robinson was the obstructive force at one end of the wicket, in his broadest pads. Somersetshire in those days was one of the country's – nay, the nation's – great humorous assets. John Daniell was captain, and amongst his co-laughers and practical jokers were Robertson-Glasgow (of everlasting and affectionate memory) and M.D.Lyon. The grim intention of Yorkshire not to score and win on the first innings, this late summer day at Bath, was too much for the comic imagination of Daniell. With only time for the bowling of two overs, he claimed a new ball. Yorkshire would take the lead (first innings) if they scored eight more runs – and lose precious percentage. Daniell gave the new ball to Robertson-Glasgow, perfect instrument in this gorgeous leg-pull of Yorkshire. He at once bowled four byes right down the leg-side, wide of Emmott's pads, right down to a bank of geraniums in front of the pavilion. Emmott was in high dudgeon, 'Ah'm surprised at you, Dr. Glasgow, usin' new ball that way'. And Robertson-Glasgow, who never missed a cue, retorted, 'That comment Emmott, coming from one who knows all, and more than all, of the uses and abuses of new ball manipulation, touches me sorely'. But Daniell, standing at mid-off and wearing an ancient brown 'trilby' hat, cried out, 'Well bowled "Crusoe". Now – four more gerania!' And again, Robertson-Glasgow sent the new ball fast down the leg-side into the flower-bed – four byes and four more 'Gerania'; and Yorkshire won on the first innings and suffered serious hurt to their Championship percentage and prospects. Here was a classic example of Gamesmanship of wit and picturesque vocabulary – 'Four more Gerania, "Crusoe",' a saying as well worth preserving historical-

BATH CRICKET WEEK.

John Daniell (left) and J.C. White at Bath, May 1920. Is the right arm gesture part of another of Daniell's jokes?

ly as Nelson's 'Kiss me, Hardy'.'

While it is certainly true that the County Championship points system described by Cardus did apply in the 1920s, the match to which he refers did not take place at Bath. It may have occurred elsewhere, but even that is uncertain. What is much more likely is that the two Somerset characters, noted for their wit, have been introduced into an incident involving Emmott Robinson where runs have been deliberately conceded in the manner described, the whole having been conflated for the purposes of a good story – and a very amusing anecdote it is.

All three principals in this story have passed away, but they were clearly great characters remembered by many with much affection. An interesting post-script to Cardus' story is provided by Humphry Crum-Ewing, a guest of Area Committee member Marc Lee, at the Bath Festival of 2000.

After Emmott Robinson retired from playing cricket for Yorkshire, he was enrolled on the panel of first-class umpires, and as such he stood in a match at the Rec in 1948. In that year, Crum-Ewing was a schoolboy at Marlborough and as a result of a special holiday having been awarded to the boys, he had spent the week-end with relatives in Bristol. On the morning of Monday 21 June, after watching Gloucestershire defeat Leicestershire by 10 wickets at Bristol, Crum-Ewing decided to return to Marlborough via Bath, where he observed play between Somerset and Hampshire during the afternoon. He remembered little of the game itself but had a vivid memory of Emmott Robinson umpiring in this match, notable for the trousers which he was wearing, which appeared to be far too big for him and sagged around the ankles. Clearly, Emmott Robinson remained a character to the end, having simply exchanged his 'broadest pads' as a player for his 'broadest trousers' as an umpire!

CHAPTER 18

'CURIOUSER AND CURIOUSER'

A CHAPTER WITH THIS TITLE must, following 'Alice's Adventures in Wonderland', introduce an element of fantasy. Inevitably, a book about cricket contains a mass of facts.While the artistry of an elegantly executed cover drive and the rhythm of a fast bowler's action may be etched on the memory of a spectator, it is the statistics of a game which are recorded in print and thereby given permanent form. But just as, in Robert Browning's words,

> .... *'Paint*
> *Must never hope to reproduce the faint*
> *Half-flush that dies along her throat...'*

so are the bare statistics unable to reproduce the full story of any game of cricket. In this Chapter, an attempt has been made deliberately to reduce, if not entirely eschew, the figures and to introduce some of the human touches lying behind the statistics.

When Sammy Woods relinquished the captaincy of the County, he had held that post for more than a decade. Born in Australia but with Somerset as his adopted home, Woods' warm personality endeared him to all in the West Country. Indeed, the extent of Woods' identification with his adopted county was encapsulated in Neville Cardus' description of him as 'a very Squire Western of Somerset cricket'. At the conclusion of play on one day of the match against South Africa in 1907, Sammy was given a gold watch as a memento of his captaincy of Somerset for thirteen seasons. It had been purchased from a Bath jeweller and it was presented to Woods by his successor as captain, Lionel Palairet. Everyone who had played for the County during Woods tenure of office as captain had been invited to subscribe to the gift.

By 1920, Woods and Palairet had long ceased playing for the County but Woods was at this time the Secretary of Somerset and he may have been among those spectators who turned up one morning in June to watch Somerset take the last four wickets to win by an innings. The Warwickshire tail-enders, however, offered stiffer resistance than expected. This surprised their own team colleagues as well as the Somerset bowlers, and when, later in the morning, Somerset batted to score the few runs required for a ten wicket victory, spectators were astonished to see half of the Warwickshire team, led by their captain, take to the field in mufti. The Honourable F.S.G.Calthorpe, who had been dismissed the previous evening, had certainly not expected to have to change into cricket clothes; nor had the Warwickshire wicket-keeper Smith, who on this occasion went behind the stumps in everyday clothes wearing neither gloves nor pads!

Playing for Somerset in that match was Mr. A.E.S.Rippon. He and his twin brother, Mr. A.D.E.Rippon, delighted in confounding all who tried to tell them apart and they had experienced mixed fortunes when they represented Somerset at the Rec in a match three weeks earlier, when each had distinguished himself in different ways. Sydney had scored a century in the first innings and carried his bat in the second, while Dudley had the misfortune to be rushed to hospital in the middle of the match with a mysterious illness which prevented him from playing any more cricket for Somerset either that season or evermore.

Bath Abbey; the fan-vaulted nave.

Numerous are the occasions when brothers have played for the same team on the cricket field. The three Grace brothers all played for England in one match in 1880 and recently, the Waugh twins have regularly represented Australia. In the late 1920s, spectators at Bath saw another pair of brothers J.W. and F.S. Lee, playing regularly for Somerset and often opening the batting together. More unusual, however, was the case in 1931, when J.W. and F.S., representing Somerset, were confronted by a third brother H.W., playing for Middlesex. In this match, which was won by Somerset, none of the Lees distinguished themselves particularly with the bat, but it was an occasion when F.S. was keeping wicket for Somerset and he stumped two batsmen, both off the bowling of J.C.White. While this was the only time at Bath that the three Lees met on the cricket pitch, there were other occasions, at Lord's and Weston-Super-Mare, when they had all played in the same match. All three were born in Marylebone; H.W., who was the oldest, played all his career for Middlesex, whereas J.W. and F.S. appeared in just one or two matches for Middlesex before coming to Somerset. F.S.Lee continued playing for Somerset after the war, but J.W., who had left to take up a coaching position at Mill Hill School in 1936, was killed in action in Normandy in 1944. Interestingly, J.W.Lee's successor as cricket coach at Mill Hill during the war was Emmott Robinson.

The bare statistic, 'Gray...Run Out....43' will not excite the reader's interest; it does, however, hide one of the more unusual dismissals of a batsman at the Rec. Hampshire, in 1957 had progressed comfortably to over one hundred runs for the loss of one wicket when opening batsman Jim Gray drove a ball from Alley so straight that it struck the wicket at the other end where his partner Horton, in anticipation of a run, had moved out of the crease. Gray, too, thinking his drive deserved a score, had begun to run. Quick as a flash, Alley picked up the ball and pulled a stump out of the ground. Horton had continued his run and Gray had decided to return towards his crease when the ball was thrown to wicket-keeper Stephenson who thereupon broke the wicket at his end, near which the two batsmen were now located. Horton accordingly walked off towards the pavillion, assuming himself to be run out, and new batsman Rayment thereupon arrived at the wicket to replace him.

It was then that spectators educated on Milton recalled those lines from 'Paradise Lost'

> '..........................Chaos umpire sits,
> And by decision more embroils the fray
> By which he reigns: next him high arbiter
> Chance governs all.'

Brian Langford batting at Bath.

For, when Horton had returned to the pavilion, he found himself being summoned back to the square. The umpires had decided that it was Gray who was run out and that it was his innings therefore which had ended. It will come as no surprise to any follower of cricket to learn that Horton was out not long after this incident. His method of dismissal? Run out !

As Gray and Horton reflected in the pavilion enclosure upon the events of the day, they probably noticed the Abbey, that majestic structure dominating the view from the Rec. Many cricketers have worshipped in Bath Abbey over the years but most are unlikely to have spent the night there. One who did do this was Peter Walker of Glamorgan. Although he had been selected for the first three Test Matches of 1960 against South Africa, and performed in them very creditably with the bat, he was having little success in his efforts for his county. In an attempt to recover his form, he decided to spend a night in Bath Abbey. While the Abbey is justly cele-

105

brated as a splendid example of the architectural style known as 'English Perpendicular', with its magnificent fan-vaulted ceiling, it is not renowned for the comfort of its pews. Not surprisingly, Walker did not rest well and, on his release from the Abbey when the cleaners arrived in the morning, he found his body aching as he walked across to the Rec. Rain delayed the start of play but after lunch Peter Walker was rewarded by an opportunity to bat. He was out for no score, or, as they say in cricket, for a duck's egg, now abbreviated to a 'duck'.

In the 1960s, the inevitable consequence of a 10 day Bath Festival (when three consecutive matches were played), was that Somerset cricketers would be playing away from home for the next one or two weeks. At the conclusion of a Bath Festival, therefore, and prior to going on tour, a player would have with him a certain amount of clean laundry for the coming games. Normally, at the end of a match, drinks were brought into the pavilion for the players. During the 1960s, it was fashionable for some to drink milk while others had the usual beer. The dressing rooms in the Bath pavilion are not spacious, and as well as containing the cricketers' equipment and 'coffins', there was a trestle table in the centre of the room. It was on this table that on one occasion, the tray of drinks was placed. Brian Langford, weary after a lengthy bowling spell, rested himself by perching on the side of this table.....and the tray of drinks, beer and milk, descended into the cricket 'coffin' of a club colleague, drenching his clean clothes for the next two weeks with an unappealing mixture of liquids!

One item of cricket equipment not in that coffin and thus 'beyond the muddy ecstasies of beer' and milk was the helmet, since this came into use only in the late 1970s. Its introduction into the first-class game necessitated a few changes of the rules. Paul Todd, opening the batting for Nottingham in 1981, thought himself dismissed when he was caught by Nigel Popplewell, fielding at short-leg. Todd was recalled, however, because the catch was made after the ball had struck Popplewell's helmet, umpire Peter Wight ruling that the ball was dead after touching the protective head-gear.

It was Nigel Popplewell who scored the fastest ever century for Somerset at Bath (see Chapter 15). This achievement, remarkable in itself, was even more noteworthy because, earlier in the Festival, in the course of a boat cruise on the River Avon, Popplewell had found himself swimming fully-clothed in the river rather than admiring it from the deck!

The soaking which Popplewell received is a reminder that all cricket is dependent on the weather. Spectators and players alike experience the frustration of matches affected by rain. It is, however, galling in the extreme when play is interrupted on account of the sun, and even more exasperating when this occurs in a match where the start has been delayed by rain. Yet this is what happened at the Rec in June 1985. Lancashire had followed on, Vic Marks had already taken one wicket, the sun was shining, and play was suspended! What happened was that the batsmen were troubled by the sun reflecting from a window in the sports centre at the North Parade end. An interruption of some 25 minutes followed while the problem was rectified by placing a large sheet over the offending window to eliminate the glare. Although eight overs were lost, when play resumed the sun was still shining and Marks was able to continue his match- winning bowling performance. And there, with the sun shining, with the type of weather of which spectators dream, and with Somerset about to claim the victory, this is perhaps the appropriate place to conclude this book written in celebration of the County's Bath Cricket Festival.

Somerset 2000. Back row, left to right: Julian Wyatt (Second XI coach), Darren Veness (physio), Piran Holloway, Matthew Wood, Jamie Grove, Stefan Jones, Peter Trego, Ian Blackwell, Carl Gazzard, Kevin Shine (First XI coach). Middle row: Mark Lathwell, Mike Burns, Greg Kennis, Ian Jones, Jason Kerr, Joe Tucker, Matthew Bulbeck, Keith Parsons, Paul Jarvis. Front row: Graham Rose, Andy Caddick, Richard Parsons (Chairman), Marcus Trescothick, Jamie Cox, Dermot Reeve (Coach), Michael Hill (President), Rob Turner, Peter Bowler.

APPENDIX 1

First-Class matches played at Bath by Somerset, with results from Somerset's viewpoint

1897	Philadelphians D.							
1898	Yorkshire	L.	Hampshire	D.				
1899	Yorkshire	L.	Kent	D.				
1900	Hampshire	W.	Gloucester	L.				
1901	Worcester	L.	Lancashire	W.				
1902	Lancashire	D.	Hampshire	W.	Gloucester	L.		
1903	Lancashire	D.	Hampshire	A.	Gloucester	W.		
1904	Gloucester	W.	Lancashire	L.	Sussex	D.		
1905	Gloucester	W.	Hampshire	D.	Australia	D.	Sussex	D.
1906	Sussex	D.	Gloucester	D.	Lancashire	L.	Yorkshire	L.
1907	Lancashire	L.	Worcester	L.	Warwick	W.	South Africa	L.
1908	Lancashire	L.	Gloucester	D.	Hampshire	L.	Surrey	D.
1909	Yorkshire	D.	Lancashire	L.	Australia	L.	Hampshire	D.
1910	Middlesex	L.	Lancashire	L.	Hampshire	L.	Sussex	L.
1911	Hampshire	W.	Middlesex	L.	Lancashire	L.		
1912	Hampshire	D.	Derbyshire	D.	South Africa	D.	Northants	L.
1913	Yorkshire	L.	Northants	L.	Sussex	D.		
1914	Surrey	L.	Sussex	L.	Hampshire	L.		
–	–		–		–		–	
1919	Worcester*	W.	Derbyshire	W.				
1920	Sussex	L.	Surrey	W.	Warwick	W.		
1921	Middlesex	L.	Essex	W.	Derbyshire	W.		
1922	Sussex	L.	Surrey	L.	Hampshire	L.		
1923	Surrey	L.	Hampshire	L.	Derbyshire	D.		
1924	Essex	A.	Derbyshire	W.	Hampshire	D.		
1925	Camb Univ	L.	Sussex	D.	Glamorgan	D.		
1926	Middlesex	L.	Derbyshire	W.	Sussex	D.		
1927	Yorkshire	D.	Sussex	D.	Glamorgan	D.		
1928	West Indies	D.	Gloucester	D.	Warwick	D.		
1929	Worcester	D.	Camb Univ	W.	Sussex	D.	Derbyshire	L.
1930	Kent	L.	Northants	D.	Yorkshire	L.	Sussex	D.
1931	Nottingham	L.	New Zealand	D.	Glamorgan	D.	Middlesex	W.
1932	Worcester	D	Yorkshire	L.	Glamorgan	W.	Gloucester	D.
1933	Northants	L.	Surrey	D.	Hampshire	D.		
1934	Hampshire	W.	Gloucester	L.				
1935	Gloucester	W.	South Africa	L.				
1936	Northants	W.	Yorkshire	L.				
1937	Worcester	W.	Kent	W.				

1938	Essex	L.	Middlesex	W.				
1939	Oxford Univ	W.	Kent	D.	Leicester	W.		
–		–		–		–		
1946	Kent	W.	Camb Univ	W.	Hampshire	W.		
1947	Leicester	W.	Camb Univ	D.	Worcester	W.		
1948	Hampshire	L.	Oxford Univ	L.	Nottingham	W.		
1949	Essex	L.	Camb Univ	L.	Middlesex	L.		
1950	Leicester	W.	Essex	W.	Lancashire	L.		
1951	Essex	L.	Hampshire	W.	Kent	W.		
1952	Middlesex	W.	Warwick	W.	Leicester	L.		
1953	Lancashire	L.	Kent	W.	Leicester	L.		
1954	Middlesex	L.	Warwick	L.	Lancashire	L.		
1955	Leicester	D.	Middlesex	W.	Warwick	L.		
1956	Kent	W.	Nottingham	W.	Worcester	L.		
1957	Hampshire	L.	Essex	W.	Derbyshire	L.		
1958	Yorkshire	L.	Gloucester	D.	Derbyshire	W.	Middlesex	L.
1959	Middlesex	D.	Leicester	W.	Yorkshire	W.	Surrey	L.
1960	Nottingham	L.	Gloucester	L.	Glamorgan	D.	Northants	L.
1961	Derbyshire	L.	Gloucester	W.	Lancashire	D.	Kent	W.
1962	Nottingham	W.	Worcester	L.	Glamorgan	W.		
1963	West Indies	L.	Gloucester	W.	Worcester	D.	Hampshire	D.
1964	Gloucester	W.	Leicester	D.	Yorkshire	D.	Lancashire	L.
1965	Worcester	W.	Hampshire	W.	Nottingham	L.		
1966	Gloucester	W.	Kent	L.	Surrey	W.		
1967	Derbyshire	L.	Yorkshire	W.	Northants	W.		
1968	Essex	D.	Hampshire	L.	Derbyshire	A.		
1969	Hampshire	W.	Gloucester	D.	Northants	D.		
1970	Derbyshire	W.	Hampshire	L.	Leicester	D.		
1971	Essex	W.	Gloucester	D.	Lancashire	D.		
1972	Northants	D.	Essex	D.	Australia	D.		
1973	Worcester	D.	Surrey	W.				
1974	Yorkshire	W.	Glamorgan	W.	Pakistan	L.		
1975	Derbyshire	W.	Surrey	D.				
1976	Middlesex	L.	Worcester	D.				
1977	Nottingham	D.	Australia	W.				
1978	Lancashire	W.	Sussex	W.				
1979	Essex	D.	Glamorgan	D.	Camb Univ	W.		
1980	Lancashire	A.	Hampshire	D.				
1981	Gloucester	D.	Nottingham	W.				
1982	Hampshire	D.	Gloucester	D.				
1983	Derbyshire	L.	Gloucester	D.				
1984	Middlesex	D.	Lancashire	D.				

1985	Gloucester	D.	Lancashire	W.
1986	Kent	W	Northants	D.
1987	Middlesex	D.	Kent	D.
1988	Warwick	D.	Sussex	D.
1989	Kent	D.	Gloucester	L.
1990	Essex	D.	Glamorgan	D.
1991	Hampshire	D.	Gloucester	D.
1992	Northants	D.	Surrey	W.
1993	Middlesex	L.		
1994	Surrey	W.		
1995	Sussex	W.		
1996	Worcester	L.		
1997	Leicester	D.		
1998	Essex	L.		
1999	Gloucester	L.		
2000	Kent	W.		

(* Match v Worcester was first-class match but did not count for County Championship as Worcestershire did not enter the competition in 1919).

Summary of Somerset results by reference to opponents at Bath

OPPONENT (COUNTY CHAMPIONSHIP)	P	W	D	L
Derbyshire	14	7	2	5
Essex	12	4	4	4
Glamorgan	9	3	6	0
Gloucestershire	26	8	12	6
Hampshire	27	8	10	9
Kent	14	8	4	2
Lancashire	19	3	5	11
Leicestershire	10	4	4	2
Middlesex	16	4	3	9
Northamptonshire	11	2	5	4
Nottinghamshire	8	4	1	3
Surrey	12	5	3	4
Sussex	16	2	10	4
Warwickshire	7	3	2	2
Worcestershire *	13	3	5	5
Yorkshire	14	3	3	8
TOTALS	228	71	78	79
Matches Abandoned **	4			

OTHER FIRST-CLASS MATCHES	P	W	D	L
Australia	4	1	2	1
New Zealand	1	0	1	0
Pakistan	1	0	0	1
South Africa	3	0	1	2
West Indies	2	0	1	1
Cambridge University	6	3	1	2
Oxford University	2	1	0	1
Philadelphians	1	0	1	0
Worcestershire (1919 match)	1	1	0	0
TOTALS	21	6	7	8

(* = excludes match (non-championship) against Worcestershire in 1919, which is included in 'Other First-Class Matches').

(**= Matches abandoned without a ball being bowled were against Hampshire (1903), Essex (1924), Derbyshire (1968) and Lancashire (1980).

APPENDIX 2

Limited Overs matches played by Somerset at Bath. Unless otherwise shown, all matches were in the John Player League (or its successor competitions, currently called the Norwich Union National Cricket League). Results are shown from Somerset's viewpoint.

1969	Kent	L.		
1970	Middlesex	W.		
1971	Sussex	W.		
1972	Essex	W.		
1973	Worcester	W.	Hampshire	L.
1974	Yorkshire	W.		
1975	Derbyshire	L.	Nottingham	L.
1976	Middlesex	W.		
1977	Nottingham	W.	Lancashire *	L.
1978	Lancashire	W.		
1979	Essex	W.		
1980	Lancashire	W.	Glamorgan	W.
1981	Gloucester	W.	Kent	L.
1982	Surrey	W.	Nottingham	W.
1983	Glamorgan	W.	Gloucester	W.
1984	Middlesex	L.	Kent	W.
1985	Gloucester	W.	Yorkshire	L.
1986	Kent	W.	Nottingham	L.
1987	Warwick	W.	Sussex	L.
1988	Warwick	L.	Surrey	W.
1989	Kent	W.	Gloucester	W.
1990	Essex	L.	Nottingham	W.
1991	Gloucester	NR	Bucks **	W.
1992	Nottingham	W.	Surrey	L.
1993	Middlesex	L.		
1994	Surrey	W.		
1995	Sussex	L.		
1996	Worcester	L.		
1997	Leicester	L.		
1998	Essex	W.		
1999	Nottingham	W.		
2000	Sussex	W.		

(* = Match played in Benson and Hedges Cup Competition).
(** = Match played in NatWest Trophy Competition).

ILLUSTRATION ACKNOWLEDGEMENTS

The author and publisher wish to thank the
following persons for permission to use the illustrations on
the pages set opposite their respective names.

Mr Bob Appleyard, Ilkley 29
Bath and North East Somerset Council 19 (photograph Fotek) 49
Bath Central Library (photographs Fotek) 15 23 31 39 54 55 73 77
Bath Newspapers 11 16 37 51 76 79 81 87 89 100
Adrian Burton, Weymouth 34 61
Mrs Elsa Buse 43 62 96
Mrs Betty Creed 69 .
Patrick Eagar, London 4 48
Robert Hale, London (Aylwin Simpson, Grounds of Appeal, 1981) 6
Hulton Archive 53
Marylebone Cricket Club 10 13
Lynn Moorhouse 7
Somerset Cricket Museum Limited, Taunton 59 66 82 91 92 95 97 105 108

Picture researcher: Susan Rose-Smith

INDEX

ILLUSTRATIONS ARE DENOTED BY
PAGE NUMBERS IN **bold** TYPE.

Abrahams, J.   36
Aird, R.   58
Alderman, T.M.   49, 92
All England XI   **11**
Alley, W.E.   23, 45-6, 72, 86, 88, **89**, 104
amateur players   38-9, 57-9, 67
Ambrose   C.E.L., 52
Ames, L.E.G.   21, 63
Amiss, D.L.   90
Amor, S.L.   59, 65, 70-1
Anderson, P.W.   19, 84-5
Andrews, W.H.   17, 61, **62**, 64, 67, 72, 90
Angell, L.   65
Appleyard, Robert   7, **16**, 17, 19, 69, **82**, 85
Appleyard, Sylvia   **16**, 17, 69, **82**, 85
Arlott, J.   42
Armstrong, W.W.   45
Arnold, R.   81
Asif Iqbal   56
Assembly Rooms   17-18
Atkinson, C.   87-8
Atkinson, G.   88
Australia
    overseas players at Rec   45-6, 49
    play at Rec   (1905), 29, 45; (1909), 15, 29,
    30, 45; (1972), 18, 46, 80; (1977), 16, 17,
    46-9, 68, 74, 80
    Somerset cricketers play for England
    against   36, 40, 41, 60

Bacher, A.   51
Dailey, T.E.   89
Bajana, M.P.   56, 57
Ball, David and Janet   14
Bardsley, W.   45
Barnes, S.F.   28
Barnett, C.J.   63
Bartlett, R.   81
Bath, Marquess of   15

Bath, Mayor of   16
Bath Abbey   **103**, 105-6
Bath Area Committee   18, 20, 80-2, **83**, 84-5
Bath Chamber of Commerce   81
Bath Chronicle   11-12, 18, 36, 40-1, 58, 63, 67, 72
Bath and County Graphic   15, 17
Bath and County Recreation Ground Co Ltd
    5, 12-13, 75-6, 83-4
Bath Cricket Club   10, 15, 18, 65, 70
Bath Herald   35
Bath Journal   10
Bath and North East Somerset Council   8,
    19, 81, 84
Bath Rugby Club (Bath Football Club)   5, 67,
    80
Bath Spa Hotel   18, 19-20
Bath Spa/Louis Powell Trophy   27
Baxter, Mrs   15
Bedminster Cricket Club   11
Bedser, A.V.   90
benefit matches   39-44
Benson and Hedges Cup   91, 94
Bevan, M.E.   98
Biddulph, K.   23
Birch, J.D.   24
Bird, H.D.   46, **48**
Birkenshaw, J.   24
Bisgood, B.L.   50
Bishop, C.   **81**, 82
Blackwell, I.   24, 27, **108**
Blanchard, J.   14, 17, 73-4
Booth, S.C.   36
Botham, I.T.   46, **48**, 55, 56, 74, 91, 95, 96
Bowes, W.E.   63
Bowler, P.   26, 44, 98, **108**
Box, T.   11
Bradfield, D.   12
Braund, L.C.   21, 22, 28, 30, 38, **39**, 40-1, 45,
    57, 65, 70
Breakwell, D.   56, 95
Brearley, W.   32
Bridges, J.J.   58, 60
Bristol   35, 87

broadcasts 17, 96-8
brochures 18-19
Bromley, William, painting by **13**
Brown, Anne 17
Brown, Derek 17, 42
Buckinghamshire County Cricket Club 5, 94
Bulbeck, M. **108**
Burgess, G.W. 46, 55, 56, 95
Burnet, J.R. 23
Burns, M. **108**
Burrough, H.D. 59, **62**, 65
Buse, Elsa 42
Buse, H.T.F. 41-2, 43, 51, **62**, 63, 65, 67, 72, 78, 86, 88, **96**
Butcher, B. 52
Buttle, C. 76

Caddick, A. 20, **24**, 25, 26, 27, 42-4, 93, **108**
Calthorpe, F.S.G. 103
Cambridge University 5, 15-16, 21, 56, 67, 87, 92
Cameron, H.B. 50
Canterbury Cricket Festival 6
Cardus, Sir Neville 99-101, 102
Carr, J.D. 74
Cartwright, T.W. 90-1
Case, C.C.C. 59, 72
Castle, F. 20, 65
Chapman, A.P.F. 63
Chappell, G.S. 18, 46, 48, **49**, 74
Cheltenham Cricket Festival 6
Chidgey, H. 50
Clarke, W. 11
Claverton Down, cricket matches 10
Clifton Cricket Club 11
Close, D.B. 23-4, 48, **49**, 56, 73, 90-1, 95
Clough, B. 18, 19
Collings, E.P. 65
commentary box 96-8
Compton, D.C.S. 90
Considine, S.G.U. 20, 35, 59, **61**, 65, 67
Cooch Behar, Maharajah of 56
Cook, S.J. 52, **97**, 98
Coombs, R. 92
Cottam, R.M.H. 88-9
Cowdrey, M.C. 90
Cox, J. 26, 49, **108**
Cranfield, B. 22, 30
Creed, L. 17, 46, 68, **69**
Critchley-Salmonson, H.R.S. 58
Crowe, M. 53, 74
Crum-Ewing H. 101

Daniell, J. 18, 28, 30, 32, 35, 40, 57, 58-9, 66-7, 72, 99, **100**

Davey, C. 77
Davis, M. 7, 18, 25
Davis, W. 40
Davison, J., painting by **19**
Day, H.L.V. 58
Delaval Astley, Capt & Mrs 15
Dennett, G. 30-1
Denning, P.W. 25, 95, **96**
Derbyshire County Cricket Club 21, 60, 89, 90
Devonshire County Cricket Club 12
Dexter, E.R. 90
Dilley, G.R. 92
Doel, E.R. 84-5
D'Oliviera, B. 46
Dorset County Cricket Club 12
Dravid, R. 25-6, 56
Dredge, C. 24, 25, 95, 96
Ducat, A. 57
Duleepsinjhi, K.S. 15-16, 56
Durham County Cricket Club 36-7

Ealham, M. 26
Earle, M. 19
Edgbaston 40
Edrich, J.H. 90
Ellison, R.M. 92
Emburey, J.E. 74
Empire Hotel 45
Endacott, J. 41
Essex County Cricket Club
    overseas players 49
    play at Rec (1919-39), 60, 64; (1951), 89; (1968), 88, 93; (1971), 90; (1979), 95
Evans, T.G. 21

Fairbrother, N. 36
Farnham, R.F.A. 85
Felix (Nicholas Wanostrocht) 10, 11
Fender, P.G.H. 35, 57, 71
Festival Dance 17-18
Festival Dinner 18, 44
Fish, Mrs 15
Fleming, M.W. 25, 26
Fletcher, K. 93
flooding 75, 77, 78, 89
Folley, I. 36
Forester, Capt 75
Fortts and Son 16
Foster, R.E. 28
Fowler, Gerald 41
Fowler, Graeme 36
Foy, P.A. 70, 71
Francis, E. 14, 18
Frederick, Prince of Wales 9-10, 18, **19**

116

Freeman, A.P.   63
Friends of the Bath County Cricket Festival
    16-17
Frost, P.   76, 81
Fry, C.B.   28
Fulton, D.P.   26
fund-raising   17-20, 84

Garner, J.   24, 25, 36, 46, 52, 74, 91, 92, 95-6,
    98
Garnett, H.G.   22
Gatting, M.W.   93
Gavaskar, S.   56, **96**
Gazzard, C.   **108**
Gerrard, R.A.   65, 67
Gibbs, L.   52
Gill, G.C.   22, 30
Gillette Cup   91, 94
Gilmer, Amanda   7
Gimblett, H.   20, 42, 61, **62**, 64, 72, 73, 78, 86
Glamorgan County Cricket Club
    play at Rec   (1932), 60; (1960), 10, 88, 105;
    (1962), 72, 87; (1974), 68; (1980), 56;
    (1983), 96
Glastonbury   87
Gloucestershire County Cricket Club
    play at Rec   (1903-8), 30, **31**; (1935), 62,
    72; (1958), 72; (1966), 87-8; (1981), 55,
    96-8; (1983), 92; (1989), 52; (1991), 52
    play Somerset (1881),   12
Gooch, G.A.   93
Gower, D.I.   93
Grace, E.M.   10, 12, 104
Grace, G.F.   10, 104
Grace, W.G.   10, **11**, 12, 28, 35, 40, 104
Graveney, T.W.,   46
Gray, J.   104-5
Greenidge, C.G.   52
Greetham, C.H.M.   23
Gregory, R.J.   71
Gregory, S.   45
Greswell, W.T.   50, 60
Griffith, C.   52
Grove, J.   **108**
Guildhall Banqueting Room   18

Hadlee, R.J.   24-5, 52, 53-4
Haigh, S.   34
Hall, W.P.   12
Hammond, W.R.   63
Hampshire County Cricket Club
    overseas players   52
    play at Rec   (1900-14) 21, 29-30; (1919-39),
    15, 41, 58-9, 63; (1940s), 21, 61, 101;
    (1957), 104-5; (1968), 78, 88-9

play Somerset (1880s), 12
Harden, R.J.   92
Hardy, N.   58
Harris, M.J.   25
Harrison, H.   35
Hart, E.J.H.   65
Hawke, Lord   33-4, 39
Hawkins, D.   **83**, 84
Hayhurst, A.N.   37
Haynes, D.L.   52, 74
Hayward, T.   28, 35, 40
Hazell, H.   20, **62**, 63, 64, 72, 86
Hearne, G.   12-13, 76
Hendren, E.H.   63, 71
Herman, O.W.   61
Hick, G.A.   56
Hill, M.   27, **108**
Hill, V.   22
Hirst, G.H.   28, 31, 66
Hitch, W.J.   35, 57, 71
Hitt, S.   **49**
Hobbs, J.B.   28, **34**, 35-6, 40, 57, 71-2
Hodgkinson, G.W.   55
Holder, R.   **7**, 17
Holloway, P.C.   26, 93, 98, **108**
Hookes, D.W.   46
Horton, H.   104-5
Howarth, G.P.   54
Humphries, H.H.   65
Hunter, D.   34
Hutton, L.   38, 42, 90
Hylton, Lord   **66**
Hylton-Stewart, B.D.   50

Illingworth, R.   22
Imran Khan   55
India   56
Ingle, R.A.   59, **62**, 65, 71
Intikhab Alam   55, 56

Jackson, A.   19
Jackson, F.S.   28
James, Mrs G.   15
Jardine, D.R.   63, 71, 78
Jarvis, P.   **108**
Jeffrey, M.   17, 18, 46, 68, 78, 84
Jennings, K.   95
Jessop, G.   30, **31**
John Player League   91, 94-8
Johnson, P.R.   28, 35, 57, 59
Jones, A.   72
Jones, I.   **108**
Jones, P.S.   26, **108**

Kapil Dev   52

Kennis, G. **108**
Kent County Cricket Club
  overseas players 49
  play at Rec (1919-39), 60, 62, 63, 67, 90;
  (1946), 21; (1951), 90; (1953), 42, 73, 77-8,
  86; (1956), 17; (1966), 88; (1969), 95;
  (1986), 68, 92; (1989), 52; (2000), 20, 25-7,
  56
  play Somerset (1884) 12
Kerr, J. **108**
King Edward VII School, Johannesburg 51
King Edward's School, Bath 20
Kitchen, M. 88

Laker, J.C. 90
Lancashire County Cricket Club
  County Championship, 1919-39, 57, 64
  play at Rec (1898-1914), 21-2, 28, 29, 32,
  65, 67, 70, **73**; (1950), 89; (1953), 42, 43,
  72, 76, 88, 89; (1954), 89; (1977), 94; (1978),
  68; (1980), 75; (1985), 21, 36, 68, 107
  play Somerset (1884), 12
Langford, B.A. 24, 42, 72-3, 78, 86, 88, 90,
  105, 106
Lansdown Cricket Club 10-12, 65, 68
Lara, B.C. 36-7
Larwood, H. 63
Lathwell, M.N. 21, **37**, 93, **108**
Law, S.G. 49
Lawrence, J. 78, 88
Lee, F.S. 51, 59, **62**, 64, 65, 104
Lee, H.W. 104
Lee, J.W. 59, 60, 64, 65, 104
Lee, Marc 101
Lee, Shane 49
Leicestershire County Cricket Club 46, 61,
  67, 73
Leveson-Gower, H.D.G. 40
Lewis, A.E. (Ted) 22, 30, **31**
Lewis, Col E.R. 15, 17, 20
Lewis, Penny 17, 18
Leyland, M. 63
Lloyd, C.H. 52
Loader, P.J. 90
Lobb, B. 90
Lock, B. **76**
Lock, G.A.R. 90
Lomax, J.G. 22, 23, 86, 90
Longrigg, E.F. 59, **62**, 65, **66**, 67, 71, 72
Lord's Cricket Ground 54, 94, 104
Lord's Taverners 16
Lowry, T.C. 54
Luckes, W.T. 59-60, **62**, 64, 71, 72
Lyon, M.D. 58, 59, **62**, 99

Macartney, C.G. 45
MacBryan, J.C.W. 20, 35, 38, 58, 59, 65-6, 67
McCool, C.L. 22-3, 46, 86
MacLaren, A.C. 21, 28, 40, 41
Mallender N., **92**, 93
Marks, V.J. 21, 25, 36, **91**, 92, 96, 107
Marsh, R.W. 46
Martyn, H. 28, **31**, 40, 45
Marylebone Cricket Club 11, 63
Masters, D.D. 26, 27
Maunder, Sybil **92**
May, C. 81
May, P.B.H. 90
Mayor's Parlour 16
Mead, C.P. 59, 63
Meddings, Ann **82**
Melbourne Cricket Club 41
Meyer, B.J. 74
Meyer, R.J.O. 86
Middlesex County Cricket Club,
  play at Rec (1898-1914), 29; (1919-39), 62,
  63, 67, 104; (1949), 90; (1954), 16, 90;
  (1955), 90; (1987), 74
Mill Hill School 104
Milton, C.A. 72
Mitchell, B. 51
Mold, A. 21, 22
Moody, T.M. 49
Moore, Ernest, painting by **29**
Moorhouse, Earl 7
Morgan, Mrs 15
Moseley, H.R. 24, 25, 52, 95
Mostyn, Mrs 15
Mushtaq Ahmed 55, 93
Mushtaq Mohammad 55-6
Mynn, A. 11, 12, **13**

Narayan, Prince 56
Nash, Richard (Beau) 9, 14
NatWest Trophy 91, 94
New Zealand 5, 50, **53**, 54-5
Newton, A.E. 34
Nicholls, G.B. 13
Nixon, P.A. 26
Noble, M.A. 45
Northamptonshire County Cricket Club
  30-1, 56, 61, 90, 94
Northway, R.P. 59, 65
Norwich Union National Cricket League 98
Nottinghamshire County Cricket Club
  Benson and Hedges Cup (1982), 94, 96
  County Championship (1981), 53
  play at Rec (1931), 63; (1948), 20; (1962),
  87; (1981), 24-5, 68, 106; (1999), 98
Nourse, A.D., senior 50

Nourse, A.D., junior 51

O'Keeffe, K.J. 49
Oldam, D. **79**
O'Shaughnessy, S.J. 36
Oxford University 5, 87

Padgett, D.V.P 23
Pakistan 5, 50, 55-6, 92
Palairet, L.C.H. 13, 15, 21-2, 23, 28, **31**, 55, 65, 66, 70, 102-3
Palairet, R.C.N. 13, 65, 66
Palmer, K.E. 87, 88, 89
Parks, J.M. 95
Parr, G. 11
Parsons, K. 26, **108**
Parsons, R. 7, **108**
Patel, M.M. 26, 27
pavilion 75
Peate, E. 33
Peel, R. 33
Philadelphians 5, 13, **55**, 56
Pilch, F. 11
Playfair Cricket Monthly 99
Pope, Alexander 9
Popplewell, N.F.M. 24-5, 92, **96**, 106
Powell, L. St. V. 17, 59, **62**, 65, 67
Proctor, M.J. 52, 98
Pulteney Meadows 5
Pump Room 18

Queen Square, obelisk 9

Racecourse Ground 11
Randall, D.W. 24
Rayment, A.W.H. 104
Redman, J. 89
Reeve, D. **108**
Regency Ballroom 18
Rhodes, W. 28, **29**, 31, 32, 33-5, 66
Rhymer, J. 19
Rice, C.E.B. 24, 25
Richards, B.A. 52
Richards, I.V.A. 24-5, 36, 46, 52, 56, 68, **69**, 91, 92, 94, 95, 96, 98
Richardson, Mrs 16
Rippon, A.D.E. 65, 103
Rippon, A.E.S. 18, 57, 58, 65, 103
Robertson-Glasgow, R.C. 54, 58, 72, 99-100
Robinson, E. 99-101, 104
Robinson, P.E. 88
Robson, E., 13 29-30, 50, 60
Roebuck, P.M. 55, 69, 91, **95**, **96**, 98
Rogers, F.E. 85
Roman Baths 16

Rose, B.C. 25, 46, 55, 91, 92, **96**
Rose, G.D. 26-7, 42-4, 93, 95-6, 98, **108**
Royal Marines Commando Forces 17
Royal United Hospital 17, 96
Royal Victoria Park, military tattoo 17
Royal York Hotel 77, 78
Ruddick, J. 38, 61
Rumsey, F.E. 88

St Christopher's School, Bath 20
Saltford 10
Sandham, A. **34**, 57, 70
Sansbury, R. 96-8
Scarborough, freedom of 40
Shafiq Ahmed 55
Sharp, J. 22
Shepherd, D. **91**
Shepherd, T. 35
Shine, K. **108**
Silk, D.R.W. 67
Simmons, J. 36
Simpson, Major 15
Sims, Sylvia **82**
Slocombe, P.A. 25, 46
Smith, E.J. 103
Smith, J. 72
Snooke, S.J. 50
Sobers, G.St.A. 52
Somerset County Cricket Club Supporters Club 17, 18, 68
Somerset U 16 team 20
Somerset Wyverns 16, 18
South Africa 5, 29, 50, **51**, 52, 60, 66; *see also* King Edward VII School
Spooner, R.H. 28
Spring Gardens 5
Squires, R 71
Staffordshire County Cricket Club 28
Statham, J.B. 72, 89
Stephens, E.J. 72
Stephenson, H.W. 24, 45, 73, 86, **87**, 104
stewards **81**, 82
Stovold, A. 98
Stringer, A. 17
Strudwick, H. 57, 70
Surrey County Cricket Club
    Benson and Hedges Cup, 94, 95-6
    County Championship (1952-5), 86
    play at Rec (1898-1914), 29, 40-1; (1919-39), 18, 21, 34, 35, 57-8, 67, 70-2, 78; (1959), 90; (1966), 88; (1970s), 54, 55, 90; (1994), 21, 37
Sussex County Cricket Club 41, 55, 56, 63, 94, 98
Sutcliffe, H. 63

Sydenham Field 11
Sylvester, Mrs 16

Tate, M.W. 63
Tattersall, R. 42, 72
Taunton 13, 29
Tavaré, C.J. 74, 98
Taylor, D.J.S. 23, 24, 25, 56, 98
Taylor, K. 73
Tennyson, L. 58
Tesser, Gianna 80
Thomson, J.R. 46
The Times 35, 74
Titmus, F.J. 90
Todd, P.A. 24, 106
Trego, P. **108**
Tremlett, M.F. 18, 20, 23, 38, 56, 72, 77, 86
Trescothick, M.E. 7, 26, 37, 93, 98, **108**
Trueman, F.S. 22, 89
Trumper, V.T. 45
Tucker, J. **108**
Turner, G.M. 54
Turner, R.J. 20, 26, 49, 93, **108**
Tyldesley, J.T. 21, 22
Tyler, E. 13, 21, 29-30, 34, 60
Tyson, F.H. 90

Ufton, D.G. 77
Underwood, D.L. 90, 92

Van Troost, A. 74
Vauxhall Gardens 5
Veness, D. **108**
Verity, H. 63
Virgin, R.T. 21, 22, 23, 88
Voce, W. 63

Wade, Major 85
Walker, M.J. 26
Walker, P.M. 105-6
Walpole, Horace 10
Walsh, C.A. 52
Walters, K.D. 46
Wanostrocht, Nicholas *see* Felix
Ward, G. 18, 81
Warner, P.F. 41
Warwickshire County Cricket Club 56, 68, 89, 103
Washbrook, C. 42, 76, 90
Watts, D. 85
Waugh, M.E. 49, 104
Waugh, S.R. 49, 104
Wellard, A.W. 20, 50-1, 59, 60-1, 62, 64, 67, 72, 86
West Gloucestershire Cricket Club 11

West Indies 5, 50, 52-3
Western Counties 11
Weston-Super-Mare 14, 87, 104
White, J.C. 32, 35, 41, 58, **59**, 60, 62, 67, 71, **100**, 104
Wickham, A.P. 70, **73**
Wight, C.V. 52
Wight, P.B. 52, 69, 72, 86, 88, 106
Wilson, D. 22-3
Wisden Cricketers Almanack 21, 29, 35-6, 39, 41, 68, 74
Withy King 8
Wood, M. **108**
Woodcock, John 74
Woods, S.M.J. 13, 15, 22, 28, 29, 45, 67, 70, 73, 102-3
Wookey Hole **53**, 54
Woolley, F. 28, 63
Worcestershire County Cricket Club 46, 49, 54, 55, 60, 61
Worrell, F. 52-3
Wright, D.V.P. 90
Wyatt, J. **108**

Yeman, P. 19, **82**, 85
Yeovil 87
Yorkshire County Cricket Club
   County Championship 22, 39, 64
   play at Rec: (1898-1914), 5, 29, 31, 33-4; (1919-39), 63, 64, 99-101; (1958), 89-90; (1959), 22-4, 73; (1974), 68, 90, 95; (2001), 8
Young A.T., 22, 37, 41, 58, 59, 60, 65, 71
Young, J. 85

Zaheer Abbas 55, 96
Zimbabwe 56

A CENTURY AT BATH
© Gavin Turner 2001
Published by Broadcast Books, 4 Cotham Vale, Bristol BS6 6HR
catherine @ broadcastbooks.demon.co.uk

Cover design by David Gould
Cover photography by Patrick Eagar
Book design by John Meek

Printed in th UK by
Cromwell Press, Trowbridge, Wiltshire